PRAISE FOR THE BOOK

"Not only is Monica Holy an excellent writer, but I was immediately captured by her personal introduction into her fascinating, but often lonely, life. I was enthralled by her insight into the spirit world, her philosophy of life and God, and her delightful sense of humor. The exhilarating discovery of 'the knowing,' 'the healing equation,' and 'ethereal bodies' in *Fringe Dweller* are concepts that will bring me guidance, inspiration, and hope always."
—Deena Budd, paranormal editor at *BellaOnline*

"*Fringe Dweller* is a humble and honest portrayal of Monica's journey in understanding and coming to grips with her incredible gift. Her writing is very timely in a world where more people are seeking answers and clarity about who we are and why we are here. It's one of those books where you forget you are reading and the story just unfolds in your mind like a movie."
—Byron Close, production manager at Corus Radio Calgary

"Monica has overridden the phrase 'fear of death' with the phrase 'embrace life.' I lost my mother in March, but now that I've read *Fringe Dweller* I've totally taken on a new attitude toward my grief. This has made a difference in my acceptance of what was a loss, but is no longer."
—Steve Bolton, professor in the Broadcasting Media Department, Loyalist College

"Monica's life purpose on earth is to assist souls to move to the other side during a traumatic death. Her ability to reach into the world of spirit and work with the souls there puts her in a league with Stuart Wilde, Sylvia Browne, John Edward, and Rosemary Altea."
—Carolyn Long, psychotherapist

"To say that Monica Holy challenges the boundaries of time and space and everything in between is an under-statement. Monica's personal insights and documentation of her other-worldly journeys in the waking, dream, and inter-dimensional states is, simply put, amazing and awe inspiring."
—Jerry Rector, author, actor, director, producer, healer

"Monica gives us a personal and extensive tour of a world beyond our fingertips; a world some of us (until now) have only caught a glimpse of. As soon as you close this book, you'll want to pick it up and read it all over again."
—Reiner Derdau, documentary film director and producer

FRINGE DWELLER
on the NIGHT SHIFT

TRUE STORIES
FROM AN AFTERLIFE PARAMEDIC

MONICA HOLY

WEISERBOOKS
San Francisco, CA / Newburyport, MA

First published in 2009 by
Red Wheel/Weiser, LLC
With offices at:
500 Third Street, Suite 230
San Francisco, CA 94107
www.redwheelweiser.com

ISBN: 978-1-57863-468-2
Library of Congress Cataloging-in-Publication Data available upon
request.

Cover design by Tracy Johnson
Text design by Donna Linden
Cover and book illustrations © Monica Holy
Typeset in Franklin Gothic and Perpetua

Printed in Canada
TCP
10 9 8 7 6 5 4 3 2 1

CONTENTS

ACKNOWLEDGMENTS

I'd like to express my gratitude to the following, without whom my story would not have been possible.

To my mother, for the first leg of my journey, whose love of books introduced me to many new worlds of unlimited potential and possibility.

To my father, whose neverending patience taught me to observe things from more than one perspective, and that where there's a will, there's a way.

To my sons, who have been my teachers of unconditional love, my connection to the "waking life." Thank you for your understanding of my leap of faith.

To Lynn, whose words "don't be afraid to be who you are" readied my flight for the second leg of my journey.

To my mentor and friend Carolyn Long, who took me under her wing and nurtured my feathers, with which I was able to soar.

For leading me to the discovery of my own inspiration, I'd like to thank Dr. Wayne Dyer.

To Glenn, who held up the mirror that challenged me to recognize where my divinity lives.

To Ellen DeGeneres, who in those dark days of blah, brought a smile to my face, started my day with an hour of laughter, and is a true inspiration to "be who you are."

Although the experiences are all mine, this book would not have been written without Hillary Wood, my ghost writer, whose patience endured the ramblings of an Aquarian mind, and whose skill wove it all together while capturing my essence.

To Ginny Weissman, who believed my story, my truth, my dreams, and recognized my intention and desire to get my story to those who would benefit from its telling.

To Nikki, who recognized a lost heart, and chose to be its guardian. Thank you for standing by me, and choosing to take this leap of faith with me, wherever it may lead.

Finally, to Jan Johnson of Red Wheel, who felt my story needed to be told. Thank you for taking this walk with me.

This journey, this book is a sum of many hearts, my gratitude goes out to all who have played a part . . . thank you.

—Monica Holy

INTRODUCTION

Sometimes I wonder where I begin, where I end. The borders by which other people seem to define themselves—their own skin, their unique circumscribed thoughts—elude me. At night I slip out of my skin and my spirit takes flight. It has always been so with me. Even as a child I didn't sleep—I went in the dark to those that called me. I call this part of my life the Night Shift, for every night a shift takes place and I move through parallel worlds, through other dimensions.

In the Night Shift, the weight of matter gets peeled back like the veil of the sun's light that hides the vast expanse of the star-filled sky. My job in the other dimensions is to work with energy—the eternal, ubiquitous source of all that is, was, and will ever be.

Science has no way—yet—to map the geography of spirit lands, or measure the weight of the souls that inhabit the spaces-in-between. And so I have no proof to bring back to the waking world. I struggle to express the ineffable freedoms and communions of spirit flight, to describe the extraordinary powers that are at play in the invisible matrix.

It is not my intent to try and convince you of the truth of telepathy, telekinesis, astral travel, life after death, reincarnation, and the existence of spirit, or to explain quantum physics. There are many fine books written on these subjects. I wish only to share my story and to allow providence to bring to it the readers who need, or want, to hear it.

I've been on the Night Shift since childhood. I grew up in a normal household filled with the ordinary demands of earning daily bread, getting children off to school, and performing accepted social roles. My family history betrayed no hints of strange powers passed from generation to generation. Our library had no books about magic, psychic ability, or the psychology of consciousness. I had no knowledge of the Eastern or Native religions that look more kindly on journeys of consciousness. I had no language to describe my experiences, and with the exception of a couple of friends in high school, no one I could talk to about them. So I learned to keep silent.

As far as those around me were concerned, the soul was something firmly lodged in the flesh, let loose from its bonds only at death. Miracles didn't happen to ordinary people; they were the doings of angels and saints. I came from a tradition that was more likely to send you off to be cured, exorcised, or otherwise returned to "normalcy" if you heard voices or saw spirits. A dweller in other worlds, I remembered harsher lifetimes in which I had felt the lick of the flames; crushing, killing blows; or the water closing over my head as I was burned, stoned, or drowned for witchery. The fear of those lives crept into this one.

There have been brief, passing moments when I've wished I had known a little about shamanism or mediumship when I was growing up. It might have helped me later, when I questioned my own sanity, or when I tried to cope with the difference I felt. I might not have felt so alone. I was determined to live an ordinary, acceptable life. I married, had children. As in any family, the demands of kids and work were a full-time job—plus overtime. I didn't have the tools then to balance and replenish my energies. Between the Night Shift and the day shift I was too exhausted to think.

Day and night pulled at each other like competing teams in a tug-of-war game. I was the middle of a taut, quivering rope, being pulled in opposite directions by teams always straining against each other. There were times when I wished it would all just go away, that I could sleep like a normal person rather than zipping around in some other dimension, helping souls to the other side, assisting in a group healing, or answering the call of a spirit in need. My children needed me too, after all.

It took several years, but one day, the day team fell into a heap, exhausted, unable to muster the energy to rise to the simplest daily task. Common objects—a spoon, a bowl—lost all meaning. I held them in my hands and could not figure out what they were for or what they were called. I felt utterly shattered. I wanted to escape from this world where our spirits are anchored so solidly in flesh, where flight is impossible, where everyone around me understands the rules of perception and matter that I seemed to have forgotten. I just wanted to give up the struggle to understand, abandon my shattered waking world, and sleep.

I had to find out whether or not I was crazy. I had to consider that the voices I heard might not be helpful spirits but the auditory hallucinations of a disordered mind, whether my night flights through other dimensions were no more than schizophrenic breaks with reality. I knew that there were many who would think so.

It was my breakdown, the shattering of all that I counted "real," that compelled me to find out. If I was going to function in the world, I had to get a grip. If it meant a life on medications, then so be it. All I knew was that I needed help.

As usual, my guides led me. I had met a therapist named Carolyn some months before, but had forgotten about her. When the breakdown came, I asked my guides what to do. "Call Carolyn," came the answer. I headed to the phone, thinking they meant a friend of mine who was also named Carolyn. "No," said the voices. "The other Carolyn." It was then that I remembered the therapist and called her.

After all the tests and questions and mental probings, Carolyn declared me sane—though I wasn't sure if that was a good thing or not. It meant there was nothing medical to cure. I was stuck with the double-shift life. My question, then, was, "What the heck is the Night Shift, if not some mental misfiring?"

"You're a medium," Carolyn said calmly, "and a natural healer." With those words my reassembly began. There were terms for what I did! As Carolyn and I worked together, many more words and concepts came to light. The breakdown turned into a breakthrough. Slowly the day team picked itself up and shook itself off. The two sides decided to end the war—though there are still spats now and then.

I don't know why I have the ability to perceive interdimensional layers of reality so clearly. Perhaps it would be of as much use to ask why some people have keener hearing than others, or a more acute sense of smell. It's just part of my nature, and could well be a part of human nature in general, buried under a blanket of disbelief so thick and heavy that the ability is, in most people, hidden even from themselves.

There is no handbook, no flight manual for the soaring spirit. If consciousness has pants, then I am flying by the seat of them. I suspect that there are many out there who, like me, perceive realities that are not apparent to those around them, and who feel isolated and strange because of it.

To you, I bring a message from the depths of my own experience:

You are not alone.
From the vast unfathomable reaches of the universe
you are not alone
From the heart of creation
you are not alone
From the hands of healing
you are not alone
From the immeasurable spaces of the in-between
you are not alone.

Your life is not a meaningless drop in the uncaring tides of history, but a work of art that you are ever in the process of creating. Your art is not a frivolous decoration, it is a divine expression of all that is.

Honor your thoughts. They are the brushes with which you paint the picture of your life.

Honor your feelings, knowing that they have the power to shape the images imprinted on the canvas of time.

Honor your imaginings. They are the pigments that bring vibrancy and color to your soul's creations.

Honor the dreams that inhabit your night hours, and the symbols they leave as gifts on the doorstep of your waking.

My guides told me to paint the image of my dreams, to get the images out there, and to detach myself from the outcome of these actions." This book began with those paintings.

Each painting is an image that holds so many layers of meaning and experience that words cannot capture them all. As I lay paint on canvas and choose the colors and forms, I wonder how the paintings can possibly convey a sense of the place, the otherworldliness, that has brought them into being. As I paint, I sense the Night Shift—even though the sun is high above. The world recedes again into dark vastness, and the whispers that guide me echo in my thoughts. I know the paintings are inadequate, that they can't explain what I see, but that doesn't matter. All that matters now is the brush, the feel of the canvas under my fingertips, and the possibility that someone will look at them, understand, be comforted by their implications. Perhaps they will recognize an image that they also have seen in the majestic journey of consciousness.

CHAPTER 1

LOVE'S LIGHT

journal entry
Monday, August 9, 2004

I am in the matrix. For me to be here means that a lost soul is ready to go home.

I have a vague corporeal structure—my ethereal body—with just enough form to appear human. I'm holding the hand of the person I'm leading. In the darkness that surrounds us, we head toward the cone of brilliant light that lies ahead. The light intensifies as we draw closer, becoming brighter than any sun that human eyes have seen, yet its brilliance does not spill out of its own form to light the space around it. The light is held within itself, waiting for the return of the spirit that approaches, waiting to bring the spirit home.

As we travel together, I feel the ineffable love that radiates from the cone of light—an overwhelming sense of peace, calm, wonder, compassion, and wellness. Our joy increases as we come yet closer, and all fear and hesitation is forgotten.

My being opens in wonder and innocence. I am free to be as vulnerable as a newborn, without fear of judgment. Waves of ecstasy wash through me and back again to the light from which they came in an exchange of pure and all-consuming love. In a fraction of a moment I know what it means to be at one with something. I am filled with a sense of connection to everyone and everything—the source of all that is.

I stop at the light's edge, still holding the hand of the soul I have led here, and gently release him into the blissful light. My hand grazes the luminosity, and every quarter of my being is pierced with the unconditional, absolute sense of infinite love that is the light.

Although I yearn to drift into the light along with the person I brought here, I know that that is not my purpose in coming, nor is it my time. I gently let go of his hand as I feel his essence begin to rise, watching in awe as he disappears into the apex of the cone before finally vanishing into the intensity of Love's Light.

He has gone home, and I am breathless with the gratitude of having come here, with the memory of my communion with eternal, limitless, infinite love.

The situation I just described will be recognizable to many readers as an account of a near death experience. It wasn't one for me because, well, I wasn't near death. Instead, I was blessed to participate as a witness and a guide as part of my work on the Night Shift.

I didn't know exactly what my job was when I got to the other side. Every time I met a soul in need, the situation was different. Sometimes the soul had already crossed over. Sometimes I took people to the light, and sometimes I just pointed them in the right direction. Sometimes I was a paramedic, or a counselor, or just a woman comforting a small child. I did whatever was needed of me, but I was confused about the role I was meant to play. I wasn't getting the overall picture.

I had asked my guides for a manual—some guidebook or job description that would make it all clear to me—but I never got one. After many requests, I met an ethereal, translucent woman, a guide, who came to respond to my frustration. "You have all you need," she said. Not satisfied with her reply, I asked again and again, but she remained patient and gentle, repeating her answer as many times as

I made the request. I never did get a manual, but I'm still busy on the Night Shift, so I guess I'll have to take it as a little lesson in trusting my guides.

One day I decided to ask my guide a different question. "What is my purpose?" I asked, and to my utter astonishment she replied, "Your purpose is to transport people to death—to help them move to the other side."

I must admit that I was horrified by the thought. This was definitely not something I could tell new acquaintances when the inevitable question came, "So, what do you do?" I could just hear the hasty excuses of a remembered appointment as they sought their escape from someone who was, at least in their books, out of her mind.

Still, it was the answer I was given, and I had to come to terms with it and get on with the job. It might have been easier to accept if I had been given the job of a more well-known type of medium—one who relays messages from those in the afterlife to those still in the material world, for instance. As it was, I would be working as a guide to the dead. There would be no evidence of what I did other than my own subjective experience, no proof that I could offer others as confirmation of my abilities. I would have to demand the utmost open-mindedness from anyone that I confided in. It promised to be a lonely and difficult road to acceptance and understanding by the world at large, and I might never achieve it. Of course, now that I've grown used to the idea, I consider it an honored position with great responsibility.

My time on the Night Shift has raised some intriguing questions about the experience of death and what happens when a soul crosses over. Why do some souls need a guide on the other side? Why, given that there is an afterlife, doesn't every soul automatically enter into the light that's talked about by those who have returned from a near death experience? And why, in the material world, doesn't everyone experience the unconditional love that emanates from the light?

There are a number of answers to the first question, most of them relating to the circumstances of death. Many people who die without warning—in an accident, or through violence—experience shock, confusion, fear, and even anger. Emotions have a vibrational frequency, and the dense, negative feelings that people hold as a result of trauma are at the lower end of the spectrum. These frequencies weigh souls down as if with heavy chains, keeping them from rising to the light. In effect, their frequencies are out of sync with the scintillations of love, serenity, gratitude, and compassion that make up the higher plane. In order to move on, these souls need to let go of the emotions that hold them back—and that's where I come in. I feel their distress and offer them my comfort so that they can release the memories of their last harrowing moments. The burdens of trauma fade away, and they are able to rejoin the light that is at the center of their true being.

As a guide in these situations, I work in the dreamtime while occupying my ethereal body. This body is able to move through the material plane as well, and as a soul transporter I'm also called by those who are close to death and need help in making the transition out of the physical body and back home to the light. Again, it is the emotions of fear, panic, and confusion that let me know my assistance is needed.

If the situation is extreme, I perform an astral maneuver called a *jump-in*. I enter the person's body, merging with them in total empathy and compassion, and giving myself over to their experience. I feel their emotions and hear their thoughts as if they were my own. I share their physical being, letting their sensations become mine. I see a chaos of images—their whole lifetime concentrated as if onto the head of a pin in a single moment. I experience their death with them. Knowing someone is there sharing their last moments on Earth is tremendously reassuring to these souls, and it eases their way to the other side.

Sometimes I'm able to help people find closure as they perform one last task before they leave the physical plane just beyond physical death and go to the light. In one such case, a young woman was mere seconds away from being murdered. I couldn't help her avoid her awful fate, but I wanted to do whatever I could to help her in her last moments and ease her way to the next.

She was in a phone booth desperately trying to call her parents to tell them she wanted to come home. Her fear was palpable. I did a jump-in, entering her body to share the emotional, physical, and mental experience she was about to have. I experienced her murder alongside her, and my spirit stayed with hers as it slipped from her body. Even as she died, the woman was calling out to her family. I took her by the hand and together we flew through the astral plane, traveling so fast that the subdivisions below became a blur of shapes and colors. When we "sensed" her parents' home, the ride came to an abrupt halt inside their house. The moment she was content that she was home again, she calmed down and vanished in a twinkling shimmer of tiny lights. With a little help, she had been able to complete unfinished business, shift frequencies, and find peace in the embrace of the light.

When two or more people die together, their main concern is often the other person's well-being. In these cases, the immediate need during and just after death is to find the other person. This happens a lot between parents and children. These situations say so much about the innate altruism and compassion of humanity. Even in the midst of the disaster and the confusion of their own deaths, these people's thoughts are of others.

In one dream, I found myself in the yard of a small harbor or yacht club. As I stood at the water's edge, a woman approached me. She wanted something, but I couldn't readily understand what it was. Instead of trying to explain, she shoved a note into my pocket. It asked me to help her find her husband and daughter. I looked up quizzically, hoping for a little more to go on, but no sooner had I caught her gaze than she unexpectedly pushed me backwards into the water.

I found myself beneath a capsized boat sunk in the murky depths. In a moment of alarm, my logical mind, ever the stickler for rules, said, "Hey, wait a minute. You can't breathe underwater." I told myself that this was dreamtime, where the rules of matter don't apply, but I still felt an urgency to find the husband and daughter the woman was looking for. I knew no one was in any physical danger (it was already too late for that), but my logical brain continued to wring its metaphorical hands. I swam from air pocket to air pocket underneath the sunken boat until I found the girl in one corner and her dad in another, but each of them disappeared instantly once I had seen them. As soon as they were gone, I found myself once again on shore with the woman who had been so anxious for my help. She mentally sent me a heartfelt message of gratitude and relief. It was now her turn to disappear. I didn't see the twinkly little lights this time, but I did feel sure that the family had crossed over together.

Before I relate the next story, I'd like to offer some comments about the relationship between the dreaming and waking worlds. In my experience, each is valid, each utterly real.

Many tend to think of dreams as private, internal events—fantasies the mind creates to release or process snippets of daily life. The waking mind hesitates to accept the reality of the dreamtime because it doesn't follow the rules that logic "knows" to be true. What takes place there is loosened from the orderly march of time from past to present to future. Matter is freed from the constraints of gravity and solidity. Yet we all sense that dreams have meaning, and that the key to unlocking the secret of that meaning lies in the symbols that we hope will help explain something of ourselves to ourselves. From this perspective, dreams are viewed as an appendage of the waking reality and the mind that perceives it. It's as if dreams are born from the material world and would not exist but for earthly experience.

Imagine, for a moment, that it's the other way around. What if waking is an appendage of the dreaming mind? What if material existence is the dream of a soul that inhabits the matrix of a wider universe of pure energy? What if our bodies, our senses, and the Earth upon which we live are symbols of our souls' dreaming?

I don't offer this exercise in imagination in order to deny the reality of the material world, but to get you to shift your thinking slightly so that you can broaden your ideas about what is real and what is not.

Dreamtime is real. In it we move through astral planes as energy, as spirits. We enter a non-material plane where feelings and thoughts rather than muscle and bone take us from place to place (if the matrix can be said to have "places"!). We are transported instantly by thought, and we communicate through telepathy—a speaking and listening that requires no words. In other words (which I *do* require here), how reality appears and operates in dreamtime is very different from how it does in ordinary waking life. So why is it that we don't wake up to our normal daily lives and remember dreams as we experienced them in our astral bodies? We might as well ask, "How does a thought look? What is the shape of a feeling?" The logical, waking mind clothes the dream elements in garments that it can recognize. The "memories" we bring back from dreams are not memories as we usually think of them, but mental constructs of the waking mind as it attempts to fit the dream experience into its own reality.

The dream world is not a private celestial room that we float through alone with only our thoughts and feelings to keep us company. It is a meeting place, an alternate dimension that we share with others. When our minds meet in that reality, we each bring feelings and perceptions to the shape of the dream. The symbols and images I give to the dream depend not only on my role in the play that unfolds on the stage of the matrix, but also on my empathetic understanding of my fellow players. As I feel the emotions of the spirit I'm with, my waking mind translates those feelings—their feelings—into the symbolic language that I speak.

For instance, in one dream I found myself in a hospital. A little boy was wandering the halls, desperately searching for his mother. His need called out to the mother in me that listens always for the cry of a lost and frightened child. As I shared his thoughts and feelings, my logical mind saw his vision of being lost as an elaborate labyrinth lined with eye-level grey hedges that surrounded us.

I took him by the hand and telepathically sent him the loving message that I would help him look for his mom. In the distance, I could hear a woman calling out for her boy. I strained to see her over the hedge, hoping to let her know that I would bring her son to her. Again, dreams are a meeting place. I could feel both his need and hers. I translated her yearning as a voice calling.

The next thing I knew we were back in the hospital's hallway. Led by the woman's voice and her desire to be with her son, I directed the boy into an elevator, which descended into the basement where bodies were kept. My reasoning mind thought this was creepy until I realized that the little boy wasn't thinking "logically" at all. He just wanted to be with his mom. The image I created was my way of understanding the situation: his mom was dead too, and she was waiting for him before she crossed over.

Still, the logical mind will have its say. I had to move beyond my natural hesitation to expose a child to the sight of his mother's body. I was glad that my image of death— a body in a morgue—was not his. His love and yearning were so focused on his mother that her image was all he saw in his mind. I pulled open the drawer where the body was kept and witnessed an astounding reunion as the intense love mother and son felt for each other swirled together in a vision of ethereal stardust before dissolving into sparkling lights. Mother and son were reunited and had gone home.

Children have a special place in my heart. As human beings, we all wonder what we could have done when we read about the shocking abuses that are sometimes perpetrated against these innocent ones. In one case, a little girl came to me lost, frightened, and shivering with shock and cold. It was clear that she had been traumatized, that her death had been truly awful. Her fear and trauma kept her bound to the plane between this life and the next. I was there to help her find the light.

I sat down, placed her on my lap, and wrapped my arms around her. I soothed her in the best way I could, stroking her hair away from her tear-streaked face and asking her name. She told me, and within moments she had calmed down. As her emotional energy shifted into this serene state, her ethereal body dissipated into a gazillion little sparkles, but not before I could feel the unconditional love that she was receiving from the other side. I later went on to read about this poor child in the news. I'm eternally grateful that her sad demise had a happy eternal ending.

In my work on the Night Shift, I come across situations that have an element of urgency to them, but the souls who call out in the moment of immediate need are not the only ones who need a guide to find their way to the light. Some souls wander for a long time, not realizing their disembodied condition. This is especially true for many of the men and women who have died in war. The soldiers I've connected with have come from everywhere on the globe and from any time in history, for war has plagued every nation and every generation.

Many of those who have died in combat appear to me after being lost for what is obviously a very, very long time by human standards. To them it may feel as if their wandering has been endless, and they long for peace. As these souls search for the homes they once knew, or for families and loved ones who once gave them shelter, they are unaware of the passage of time on Earth. They can't understand why everything looks different, why their homes are gone. It is as if the sudden and traumatic nature of their death has fixed their awareness to a specific time and place that they can't let go of. Their consciousness is still directed at the world they knew. When I meet these souls, I explain to them that those they are looking for are waiting for them in another place, and that they must look elsewhere to find them. After speaking with me, they are able to turn their awareness in another direction, accept their passing, and go to the light's embrace where they find at last the loved ones who wait for them there.

As a result of meeting these soldiers, I've developed a keen interest in history and a habit of watching documentaries and films about war. It is often useful for me to be able to recognize the uniforms and weapons used through history so that I can understand what war my lost soldier souls were in, and perhaps a little of what they went through. This way, I'm better able to relate to them and their circumstances at death. You must understand: when I'm in ethereal form and on the Night Shift, I carry the part of my mind that is oriented to ordinary daily life with me. As in any job, it helps to be informed, and the more information I bring to the Night Shift, the better I'm able to communicate with a soul that is lost.

As we die, the process of letting go is not always easy. Many souls carry the limited, familiar beliefs and thoughts of their earthly lives to the other side, holding on to them for a time before they are ready to experience the endless possibilities and the ineffable, unconditional love that awaits them. They cling briefly to the idea that they are not part of the divine, creative compassion that shapes the universe. With guidance, though, they can change frequencies away from the heavy emotions that keep them from realizing that they are one with the light.

This is as true here as it is on the other side. Love's Light is available to us even in this earthly life. You can find evidence of it in ordinary moments of your day. It's simple: you see what you choose to look at.

If you look only at the dark—the painful episodes in your life, the acts of violence and cruelty around you— you begin to construct blinders of cynicism, distrust, and fear until a bleak picture is all that you see. This outlook is no different from that of the soul weighed down by the shackles it carries to the other side. Here or there, we disconnect ourselves from Source when we stop noticing the light of love and compassion that is all around us.

Reconnecting to Source is not difficult. Take notice of the sparks of joy, beauty, and gentleness in your waking life. Remember the kind word of a stranger. Watch a butterfly as it alights on a rose. Listen to the delighted laughter of a child as he kicks his way through the vibrant beauty of autumn leaves fallen on the sidewalk. Shift your awareness. These moments exist all around you all the time; you need only look for them. Grasp them in your mind and you will begin to feel the love that is around you, waiting patiently to be noticed.

Each time I see a spirit become one with the light, I am assured of the omnipresent nature of love. I do whatever I can, in this world and on the other side, to point souls toward it. However, since much of my work on the Night Shift is a matter of popping into a story in progress and then leaving it when my part is done, I've found it frustrating to not know whether or not my spirit work has made a difference. Like a movie interrupted, I don't get to see the ending. Do all the souls that I've guided to the light actually make it? I know I've led them there, but despite all my experience, I still have the occasional doubt.

Pondering this question one day, I decided that proof didn't matter. What mattered was the act of compassion itself. Love was its own validation. I set the question aside, satisfied with the answer and prepared to live with not knowing.

That night, I was in ethereal form but traveling in the material plane. I found myself on a cement embankment by a river. It was dark, and I could barely make out the human figure before me. He was in his late 30s, although life as a drug addict had left him looking much older. I knew he would need help crossing over.

I could sense his body shutting down. Years of chemical abuse and poor nutrition had taken their toll. He was on the verge of death, but his sad life was not yet free of abuse. His drug dealer was also present on the embankment, and I could feel the dealer's dark intent to light his victim's body on fire and dump him into the river below to avoid identification. The addict knew, too, and in his last moments, he called out to anyone, anything, for help—for an end to his pain.

His body had suffered enough. Although I was there in my ethereal form, I realized I had to find a way to interact on a physical level since he was still in waking reality. I did a jump-in, merging myself with him. I felt all the pain and sorrow that had brought him there, all the regret of someone who had looked for some small joy in the wrong places—the crack pipe and the needle. The man was already dying; my only concern was to let him die with some small measure of the peace that had eluded him in life. I concentrated all my energy to roll him down the embankment and into the water before he was subjected to any more cruelty. I turned him on his back, face-up, so that he could breathe, and pushed us as far away from the dealer as possible. We floated for a while together, drifting around the river's bend and into the bay, before I jumped back out of his body. I stayed with him, treading water, knowing I couldn't do anything more for him at that point.

Then I let him go. I remained in the water, watching him drift out of sight, but not before he up-righted himself and gave me a wave of farewell. He was so close to death that he could see my ethereal form. He knew that he was headed for a better place, and did not need me to lead him into the light. I knew he would find his own way there.

I assumed that, like all the other times, this would be the end of my story with a soul in transition, but that turned out not to be so. I was back in the ethereal plane when suddenly the scene shifted. It was midday, bright and sunny, and I found myself on shore a little way up from the river's edge. I noticed a man floating by, and saw that it was the drug addict. He was actually swimming, and I realized that he had actively been looking for me. He had returned after crossing over to find me in the dreamtime. I walked towards the shoreline as he came in from the water and offered me a note with a map telling me how to find him. I accepted the map, but knew I didn't need it in order to locate him on the other side. I'd got his number, so to speak. Instead of reading the map, I chose to walk with him back into the beautiful clean river for a further explanation, wondering what he was doing here now that he had crossed over. He grabbed my hand and led me further into the water and around the river's bend, to a quiet place out of sight.

I was stunned by the vibrancy of his essence and the look of his perfect body. He was completely "cleaned up," and could have passed for a very handsome European soccer player. He was gorgeous! Although he was not wearing clothing, he was enrobed in glowing vitality. Never before in my experiences had anyone come back like this. Hadn't he made it to the light as I had thought? Sensing my confusion, he wrapped his arms around me in a warm embrace and sent me the thought, "It's what you need right now."

I was exhausted and he held me afloat, just as I had held his face above the water in his last moments. I felt him infusing me with unconditional love and renewing my spirit before he left me. The proof I had so longed for and that had seemed so important to me felt inconsequential then. More gratifying was witnessing how a person could leave this life a physical and emotional wreck and in a heartbeat come back in a state of soul perfection.

This young man's story illustrates to me that no matter how many mistakes we make in life, when we die we are embraced, made whole and healthy, and restored to the light that is at the core of our being. There is no eternal damnation waiting. Guilt is washed away in the light of unconditional love and forgiveness that is the essence of Source.

There is no need to fear death. If you are ill, hurt, or in pain, you can look forward to a perfect state of health, youth, and vitality on the other side. Pain does not exist there—but love does.

If you have lost a loved one, a spouse, or family member, you can be sure they're waiting to welcome you on the other side. Even beloved animals are waiting there for you once you've crossed over. When you die you experience a homecoming.

I've been present when someone close to death has had loved ones come to greet her even before her passing. This was the case when my grandmother, who I called Oma, passed away. I saw her lying on her deathbed, surrounded by figures from the other side. When I later described these figures to my mother, she recognized one of them as my grandmother's best friend, who had died forty years earlier in a train accident. How wonderful it was that my Oma was reunited with her long-departed best friend!

A year after I had the dream that led to the painting of *Love's Light,* I had a similar one that drew me again to the incomparable beauty of Source. I was on a snowy mountaintop, hovering in ethereal form. I felt my being attracting elements and energies with ever-increasing strength until they swirled around me like a vortex. The sheer energy of it built to hurricane force, and I began to fly upward toward the sun, speeding past the celestial orbs suspended in space. I felt like a moth drawn to a flame, intoxicated by the all-encompassing love that beckoned. I was going home. Then, halfway to the light, I thought, "No, there's too much work still to do." I made the decision to return and continue my work on the Night Shift, knowing with complete certainty that what awaits me awaits us all when our time here is through.

CHAPTER 2

THANK YOU

journal entry
Thursday, April 30, 2004

Exhausted, I lie on my bed, asking "What's next, what's next?" in a habitual litany. I've been asking that question for the past four months, since I saw my friend Lynn through her last days before she died of cancer. I've also been working through the nights for months, led and taught by the light beings that help me in the energy healing, and through the days to see to Lynn's physical needs. And now that it is over, the question echoes as if I have not quite let her go, as if there is something more that needs to be done.

I realize what it is. I have forgotten to thank all of those who came to help and teach me—the beings that exist on another plane, in another dimension, and bring their tireless and infinite love to the energy work. They had come to me in dreams with diagrams and charts, showing me where to lay my hands, how to direct and apply my energy. They had offered suggestions for diet and homeopathic remedies. They had given me love, guidance, and support through every minute of the emotionally intense journey that I had been on with Lynn.

I am filled with gratitude, brimming with thanks for all that I remember of those days and nights. Suddenly, the room begins to fill with spirits—beings of light—pouring love into me and the air around me. There seem to be hundreds of them.

For a moment, doubt makes me ask, "Is this really happening? Can this happen in waking hours?" But my doubt is put to rest by the evidence in front of my own eyes, and I see how the light emanates from their hearts, the infinite compassion shining on their faces. They float above the ground, swaying as gently as seaweed does in the ocean's tide. Whatever doubt I have is absorbed and set aside by the physical joy I feel in every cell of my body as gentleness and love lift me out of time and into the worlds beyond— the soul's home.

As one, the light beings raise their right arms and wave as if to say, "It's all right that you forgot us. And you're welcome," in a gesture of infinite generosity.

The daylight appearance of spirits is rare for me, but it happens now and then, just as it did on that afternoon three days after Lynn had gone. Perhaps it is because I've learned to let down the barriers between the Night Shift and waking hours that the spirits came to me that day, slipping into my consciousness on the thread of the memory of what they had done and what Lynn had meant to me.

Lynn had been one of my two best friends in high school. We called our trio the Three Amigos, and we told each other everything. Nikki and Lynn were the only two that I had confided in about the Night Shift. I met them when I was in the twelfth grade and they were in the ninth. I didn't say so at the time—by then I was cautious about revealing my hidden and baffling nightlife—but I recognized Nikki the moment I met her, for I had seen her in visions years before. Her face as I saw it in the visions was not the fourteen-year-old Nikki but rather her as an older woman, as she is now, at the time of this writing.

I lost track of my two friends after I got married and tried to make a life that didn't include the strange and alienating experiences that I had shared with no one else. I closed the door on the Night Shift as if I could deny my own nature, dismiss what I was. Divided against myself,

I had fallen apart. The story of my struggles in the years between disintegration and reconstruction is a long one, and I will not relay it here. It is not the struggle that counts but the learning that comes of it—the return to love that is its message.

In the long, lonely years—nearly twenty of them—since I had seen my friends, I wondered if I could ever again find the understanding and acceptance I had known with them until one day, at the height of my despair, I asked for help for my ailing spirit, and I was answered. Destiny, synchronicity, or whatever name you give the forces that gather to direct our lives where they need to go, led me to Carolyn Long. She became my mentor and gave me the tools to manage my lives. With her, I learned to accept and work with the energies that had been given to me. We used, among other things, the journey process to uncover memories and free emotional blocks that had built up over the years. In the year I spent working with Carolyn, I entered a new life phase, armed with the tools necessary to cope with the unusual gifts that defined my reality.

In my work with Carolyn, I was able to recall another incidence of the daylight appearance of a spirit that I had long since forgotten. I was ten or eleven. On that particular day I was alone in my room, daydreaming, when I got the feeling that something *big* was about to happen. The hairs on my body began to prickle with the sense that someone, or something, was in the room with me. Looking around, I saw a life-size being appear out of nowhere. He (for I knew it was a he) was wrapped in glowing bands of light, and floated inches off the ground. I could hardly believe my eyes, didn't *want* to believe them, but there he was—and he was heading right for me. I couldn't move, even though I wanted more than anything to get up and run for my life. My body and brain were completely paralyzed.

The being must have sensed my terror. "It's okay," he said. "I won't hurt you. You have nothing to fear." The words didn't sound like normal speech, but more like the echo of a thought inside my head. I was oddly reassured by them, and even began to feel a tiny bit of curiosity about this strange, unearthly soul—enough to allow myself to peer into his eyes. They were the eyes of one ancient beyond reckoning, wreathed in brown skin so wrinkled that it looked as if it had been gouged by the experience of countless millennia. I saw in their sparkling blue depths a bottomless well of love, compassion, and wisdom. I knew then that this entity wouldn't hurt me, but still a part of me hung on to my fear.

I mentally gulped and watched as he gingerly stretched out his fingers toward my forehead, halting only a touch away. Suddenly, a stream of light coursed into my mind like an electric current, surging so fast that I caught glimpses of blue strands arcing through the air from his fingertips into my head. I felt as if my mind was a reservoir and that he had turned on a tap of knowledge so vast and ancient that the human brain could not comprehend, only succumb.

Along with this torrent of information came a sense of infinite, boundless love. It seemed to go on and on until, just when I thought I could bear no more, it stopped. I lay absolutely stunned, but the spirit merely held both hands outstretched toward me with his palms up and said, "Here is a gift. Use it well." With that he was gone. I called him Good Eyes.

With Carolyn's help, I recalled that visitation. It seemed like it had occurred a lifetime ago. I remembered what I had known since I was a child: that I had been sent a gift, and gifts are meant to be shared. I have been called on to answer souls in need, to help them according to my ability, however strange or unusual it seems.

During my work with Carolyn, I had gone a long way in coming to terms with what I was, what I could do, and my decision to honor the request of Good Eyes. In addition to learning how to marshal and direct my energies with meditation and visualization, I found out how to ground and protect myself. I honed the tools of focus and intent. I began to work with the beings that entered my life on the Night Shift to heal in the places hidden deep within cells and molecules. I came to trust myself, and to be courageous in my exploration of the layers of reality and consciousness that were the offices of the Night Shift. I started to read about cultures that understand and re-spect the role of spirit in the material world. I found some resonance with my experience in the books of modern spiritual teachers. At last I committed to using the gift that had been placed in my keeping.

Things in life happen when they need to, when our spirits are ready for them. They happen through synchronicities and revisitations to truths that we must face if we are to grow.

And so it happened that at just the time when I had learned to accept, trust, and explore my strange gift without fear, I got a call. It was Nikki. I hadn't seen her or Lynn in twenty years, but the three of us hadn't forgotten the special bond we had formed. Now, out of the blue, our paths met again.

"Lynn is dying," Nikki said. "We need you here." What eventually came out of those simple, direct words was a reordering of my life and another step on the journey that had apparently been set for me since before I was born.

The four months I spent with Lynn at the end of her life here on Earth led to the vision that I painted and later named *Thank You*. The experiences of those months and the vision that came soon after them have inspired many of my thoughts about the nature of time, healing, gratitude, love, being, and death.

I believe in the eternity of the personal spirit with all its quirks. How could I not? I have worked with spirits in the process of crossing over many times. They worry about their loved ones here on Earth, are frightened or confused by their new disembodied condition. They have needs and distinct personalities—unique essences—that are theirs from life to life.

Reincarnation goes unquestioned by many cultures. People of the Buddhist and Hindu faiths, for example, believe that we return many times to earthly existence. Like them, I don't question reincarnation. I've had many alternate lives appear in my dreams, and I know them by a particular feeling that marks them, like a recognition of a place I've been before.

My first memory in this life was that of my death in another lifetime. In that life, I was a man in the middle of a war. My comrades and I had been fighting our way through a dense, steaming jungle for days. We stopped, exhausted, and sat down to rest, but more than anything we wanted to take off our boots. My feet felt like stumps of burning pain encased in the unforgiving heavy leather. Along with my fellow soldiers, I unlaced my boots and gingerly pulled them off. My swollen feet were covered with open sores and blisters, like those of my comrades. I wondered how we could stuff them back into the boots that seemed now like so many instruments of torture strewn in the small clearing.

Suddenly, I heard a sound like a small click. I looked up to see a rifle with bayonet attached pointed right at me. We were surrounded. As the Asian soldiers came out of the jungle with their weapons leveled, we put up our hands in surrender and slowly rose. My heart was pounding. One false move could mean death.

With guns and bayonets, the enemy soldiers indicated that we should march ahead of them into the jungle. I knew that, wherever we were headed, we would need our boots. I pointed down to my bare feet and over at my boots, asking by gesture if I could put them back on. I thought the enemy understood, but as I reached down, they opened fire. In that concentrated moment, the bullets seemed to creep through the air. I watched every millimeter of their progress in the heightened awareness that seized me. I felt them as again and again they ripped through my uniform and into my body. The final bullet slammed into my forehead, throwing my head back in an explosion of force. Everything went black.

I had that dream before I could walk, and have had it many times since. The jungle setting, khaki uniforms, and cloth caps of the enemy soldiers suggest that it was a scene from the Korean War.

I've had other recurring alternate-life dreams and wondered if the repetition was a way for me to release my feelings about the incident in some way. Like a traumatic experience, the memories of disturbing events from other lives come through again and again until they are resolved.

One of these involves Nikki. In that incarnation, I was a man, and Nikki and I were a couple. Details of the dreamscape suggest twentieth-century Germany during wartime. As the dream began, Nikki and I were together at a train depot. The atmosphere was charged with a kind of hypervigilance, a guardedness. A woman approached and asked me to identify two men, whom I pointed out to her. The woman then went into a bathroom, but the interaction had made me uneasy. I "felt" that she had the murder of these two men on her mind. My unease was confirmed when, standing just outside the door, I overheard her hatching a plot with someone who had met her inside the damp and ill-lit room. I drew Nikki to the door so that we could listen to the details and decide how to derail the woman's nefarious plans. She must have realized that we were on the other side of the door, because she suddenly whipped it open and pulled out a gun. I shoved Nikki away to the right as I stepped left to duck around a corner. The woman stepped forward and around, raised the gun, aimed, and shot me—all in a split second. She disappeared as I fell, bleeding, to the ground. Nikki rushed to my side.

The next thing I knew, Nikki and I were in a snow-covered field. Icy rain was pouring down, and somehow I knew that the closest doctor was miles away. We struggled in the direction of the nearest town, but it seemed hopeless. Nikki was holding me up, almost carrying me, as I grew weaker and weaker with my gunshot wound. When I could go no further, she was forced to leave me on the frozen ground as she continued on to find help. The dream ended as I waited for her to return. She may not have been able to make it back in time to save me then, but in the infinite possibilities of the matrix it is never too late. She has come back in other lives to help me through critical moments. We can choose to return in one life to fulfill the promise of another.

Interestingly, I've also met Nikki's father in other lives. I barely knew him in this life, but that was not always so. He was my comrade-at-arms in the Roman army. He was bulky and solid, and older than me, who at the time had twenty and some odd years under my belt. We had watched each other's backs through many a battle and shared the trust and camaraderie of fellow soldiers.

As the dream began, we were walking toward a tent. We had come in answer to a note challenging us to a hand-to-hand battle: the two of us against two soldiers from an opposing army. It was a matter of honor to go. We carried with us the small shields and short swords of personal combat.

We reached the tent where we were to meet our challengers, lifted the flap, and entered. It was dark and empty inside. We wondered where our foes were—surely they wouldn't have abandoned the fight and their honor with it. Suddenly, we knew. Our eyes met and our hearts plummeted. There would be no honor here, only cowardly ambush and probable death born from the cold, impersonal heart of politics. We had walked into the scene of our own assassination.

As quickly as the thought flashed between us, two arrows pierced the tent. We barely had time to fall to the ground and raise the tiny shields for what small protection they could offer us when a torrent of arrows assaulted us from every side. I heard the snick, snick, snick of the tent's fabric as it was torn by the slender, deadly shafts that rained down on us in what felt like an eternity of onslaught.

Suddenly, all went quiet. It was over. Miraculously, I had survived. I looked up into the utter silence and saw only the dust motes dancing in the narrow beams of light that criss-crossed the interior of the tent. Nikki's father, my comrade and mentor, lay dead. I like to think that the lights of his spirit danced in the matrix like those silvery motes until they coalesced again to form the man I knew as Nikki's father.

I've lived as both a man and a woman in many countries and continents. I've worn the skin of different races. No doubt I've met many of the people I know in this life at other times and in other places. This is true for all of us as we enter the material world in various incarnations: we experience different configurations of relationship with each other, exploring possibilities of interaction with one another. In another lifetime your mother may have been your son, for instance, or your best friend may have been your sister.

I had a dream that described reincarnation in a beautifully simple way. I was sitting with a man in the future, looking at a catalogue he was proudly showing me that was filled with photos of his dream car. He then pulled out another catalogue of photos showing interchangeable parts for the car. Each person, he explained, has a base car—a vehicle that remains the same. Only the look of the vehicle changes, depending on what parts are chosen to adorn it. Adornments are adapted to time and place. Simple! And with very interesting implications: we choose how to present ourselves to the material world. What we are when we come into life—however many times—is not a reward or punishment for unremembered events in other times, but an opportunity to broaden our knowledge of ourselves.

In another dream, I was shown a beautiful representation of what each individual's accumulated physical lives might look like if we could see them. The cerulean sky was full of flying totem poles, each one different, reflecting the individual and unique essence that is each of ours through eternity. Each figure carved on a pole and each brightly colored band that circled it represented a different life. Each totem pole had two sets of wings. One pair was made out of wood, a symbol of Earth and the waking reality, and they jutted out to the side. The others were larger, white, and feathered, fixed behind the wooden ones. They were symbols of the dreaming, nocturnal reality. It was these larger white wings that carried the totem poles aloft into the clear sky. Our spirit traverses both waking and dreaming realities, and our totem is the art we make of ourselves, carved out by the tools of action, emotion, and intention. Each stroke of the chisel expresses and modifies our creative essence as we master our skills. I found this dream particularly lyrical.

I've come to believe that we come into each life with a chart—a list of experiences we wish to have while in an earthly incarnation. As well as choosing gender, historical period, and other circumstances, we invite challenges or hardships into life in order to learn from them. Sometimes these include disease or illness, which can be powerful motivations to look within where the meaning of our lives resides. I don't consider this chart to be a written-in-stone predestination. We are presented with the experiences we've charted out before incarnation, and how we respond to those experiences is a matter of free will. We come into the material world to develop and evolve our souls, and we do so by responding to events and then reflecting on our own actions, thoughts, and feelings.

In each incarnation of life, we have exit points—times we can choose to die (or not). Birth and the moment of death are matters between our highest selves and our creator. No one else can override this covenant. No one can choose for us when we will be born or when we will die. Part of our education is to come to the understanding that we are not victims of random circumstance. Events do not happen to us without our complicity. Each time we choose to return to Earth, we do so in order to learn more about our covenant of co-creation.

The people that come into our lives do not do so randomly, either. We invite them in, and we learn together in our house of earthly education. We are all part of each other's story. Sometimes disease is a character, and the ripple effect of our living with and perhaps dying from a disease plays a part in someone else's life. This is a part of the story also—a way in which we can teach each other about tenderness, healing, and love. Personally, I have a great deal of compassion for those who write disease into their chart, for through their adversity they create a path to challenge their growth and ours, too.

On the day following Lynn's passing, I had to question the purpose of my energy work. It could not save my friend, and I felt that her death was my failure. But from the spirit perspective, death is a moving on, a next step in the soul's journey. It is a choice to come to Earth, and a choice, when the time comes, to go. Healing is not meant to save souls from their own journey, but to help them along their unique path. Earthly life cannot be forced on an unwilling soul. Perhaps Lynn had come back into my life to teach me this very thing. Whatever mourning I did for Lynn was tempered by the knowledge that death is a flowering of consciousness into a unified reality.

Before she left this life, Lynn let me know that what we were doing on the Night Shift was having an effect. I hadn't told her about the energy healing I was doing at night, but one day she said, "I remember waking up last night and seeing a group of light beings around me, giving me energy. And one of them said, 'Go back to sleep. We're not done working yet.'" She cannot have known how much her words helped me later to set aside my doubts and believe that I was achieving something on the Night Shift—and that others were helping also. Or perhaps she did know, and that's why she told me—another one of the gifts that she gave me during those days.

After Lynn had crossed over, she came to me in another waking experience. A couple of nights after she had gone, I was walking up the stairs toward my bedroom. Suddenly, as I approached the door, I felt the temperature change. A chilly air flooded out of my room, signaling the presence of a spirit. Passing through it, I collapsed onto the bed.

As I lay there looking at the ceiling and shivering, I started questioning the experiences of the past four months. "Was it all a coincidence?" I asked. "Did I really make any difference? Was the whole thing my imagination?" As I pondered these questions, my shivering changed to a vibrating calm as I shifted to a state of waiting expectancy. Staring at the ceiling above the bed, I saw a spot of light, which started to grow until it was a glowing circle above me. It pulsated with the gentle green of healing and new life, like the color of a young leaf unfurling in spring. Suddenly a beam of light from the center of the circle descended straight into my heart. All of the healing love, warmth, and energy that I had directed at Lynn came back to me in that moment and I heard her say, "This is for all the light you filled me with. Now I am returning the act." My entire body surged with warmth and love. I have never felt that much love before . . . ever. I sensed my consciousness merging with hers in a perfect communion that went beyond empathy, beyond telepathy, and out into the infinity of One.

Later that night, I dreamt of a phone ringing. I picked it up to hear a voice say, "Lynn on line one." Apparently Lynn had gotten a promotion; she now had a secretary with a touch-tone phone. She had called to tell me that she had "returned to wholeness."

The days and nights that I spent with this friend who reached out to me in her final moments taught me more than any guru or religion could have about the infinity of love and the truth of my experience. The series of paintings that I offer you began with the understanding and trust that she offered me. So thank you, Lynn. Thank you so much for your confirmation and your continued communication. You know I won't forget you and I know you won't forget me. Namaste. May we meet again in another life. In the meantime, feel free to call any time.

CHAPTER 3

THE FLACKER

journal entry
Tuesday, February 14, 2006

It's a pleasant social moment in dreamtime. I'm telling a story to a friend about the escapades of my Burmese cat battling it out with a squash.

A sound intrudes from the background. It's faint at first, but as it gets louder it starts to annoy me. It's like the stutter of fingers being rubbed on an inflated balloon and rates right up there with nails scraping on the surface of a chalkboard. I shiver involuntarily.

Doing my best to ignore the distraction, I carry on with my tale, but the noise is persistent and gets louder yet. "Don't you hear that?" I finally ask my friend, but she claims not to have heard a thing. Shrugging, I pick up the thread of the story a third time and just as I begin again, I become aware of a ghostly presence out of the corner of my eye.

It's a young woman–perhaps in her late teens– wearing blue jeans and a long-sleeved blue striped shirt. She's soaking wet. Her long, straggly blonde hair is plastered in matted strands against her face. Her face is gaunt. She looks as though she's drowned. I feel her close now, standing just by the bedside, but I refuse to give up my story, anxious to get to the punch line.

Suddenly her form begins to flicker back and forth like the strobing image from an old film projector. Between the flickering image and the stuttering sound, it's nothing short of creepy. My patience at an end, I finally give in and turn to her. "Stop it!" I demand. "You're freaking me out!"

"Well, I got your attention, didn't I?" she says, smiling slightly in apology.

"Yes," I admit, "but it freaks me out, so please stop doing it!"

"It's called flacking," she replies, and with that she disappears. Although she hasn't told me her name, I know it is Debbie.

Not all ghosts communicate in the same way or for the same reasons. A call for help from a lost soul will be very

different from a friendly visit—or a plea for acknowl-
edgement, which is what I was getting from Debbie, the
flacking ghost.

The sight of Debbie's lurching, shadowy form would
have been more frightening if I hadn't learned long ago
to trust my intuition about the spirits I encounter. I knew
that Debbie meant me no harm; she had merely chosen a
rather unusual and dramatic way of getting my attention.
A moment of my time and attention was all she needed,
so she used the ghostly equivalent of a child plucking at a
grown-up's sleeve in the middle of a conversation. Once
satisfied that I had noticed her, off she went.

We all remember the delicious shivers of a good ghost
story delivered around the campfire or in a darkened
room as a storm raged outside. Those stories form a part
of most people's tradition. Literature, art, and film carry
the tradition forward. The ghost story never dies.

Even if we give up those stories when we come to
adulthood, we carry from them a number of questions: Is
there life after death? And if so, can there be communication between the two worlds? Are there portals from one
world to the next? How do we enter them? These questions are important. The answers shape our worldview,
and our worldview in turn shapes our experience.

Many, many people—perhaps the majority of humans—believe wholeheartedly that there *is* life after
death, that there are doorways between realities, and that
communication with ghosts is possible. Of course, I am

one of them. My experience has led me irrevocably and enthusiastically to that conclusion.

Ghostly encounters are rarely fearsome. Nonetheless, many people feel a fright on their first encounter—if it happens when they're awake. Meeting a ghost can be a life-altering experience that opens a door to a new understanding of who and what we are. No matter what the message from the other side, the fact that there *is* a message changes our perspective on ourselves and our world.

People give many names to ghosts—apparitions, spirits, souls, entities. Ghosts are disincarnate spirits who for one reason or another interact with our physical realm. Sometimes they have a specific message, or their appearance may be a sign that they have something to resolve, some unfinished business. We think of sorrowful things when we think of ghosts: sad endings, beings that come back to haunt people or places that were important to them in life. Ghosts are quite often attached to a place—be it a house, a room, a street, or even an open meadow where they once walked with their sweetheart. Many Indigenous cultures believe that it is important to bury one's remains in the soil of their homeland. If this is not done, the ghost may revisit its descendants, haunting them, in effect, until the body is brought home and laid to rest in native land. When people are especially attached to the land, burial in a foreign place can be distressing to the spirit and prevent passage to the light on the other side.

Ghosts who feel they have unfinished business may revisit Earth to resolve it. For instance, a person who was attached to ceremonies and rites in life may not want to go if they feel they have not received a proper burial. This is not so much about attachment to a particular burial place as it is about the rituals that accompany death. It may take no more than the words of a priest or relatives' loving wishes and a small ceremony to send the spirit on its way.

Some ghosts cling to a person or relationship they remember from their incarnation. They come back again and again to revisit their earthly attachment. They haunt and are haunted by the memory of the relationships of their physical existence.

A haunting is a sign that a ghost cannot move on yet. The haunting ghost is not in emergency mode; it is in a state of mourning, and the sorrow of mourning is one of the most difficult emotions to give up. It binds us to the past and often to regret about that past. It has a tinge of sweet nostalgia, a yearning that is almost like hope. That's why it is so hard to give up. There is something gentle in it, something that says it could have been better if only we had known more. Our imaginings of what could have been are our haunting, and such yearning may keep ghosts, as well as humans, from moving on. A spirit may hang around to apologize to those he thought he hurt in life. Often enough, a good dose of forgiveness or the assurance that he can come back in another incarnation to make a better job of life will finally send him on his way.

Not all ghostly visits are as sad as they may sound, because not all ghostly visits are hauntings. Sometimes ghosts ride back to our reality on a thread of love, hoping to see how things are going. My Grandma comes by every once in a while to say hello and see how the family is doing. She dropped into one of my dreams soon after she had passed.

I walked into a family gathering and saw Oma standing next to my mother. I didn't recognize her at first, because she was wearing an outfit she never would have worn while she was here. It reminded me of something from the closet of Queen Elizabeth—a light sky-blue blazer and skirt with a matching wide-brimmed hat trimmed at the edge with white lace. As I approached, I noticed Oma's bright smile and amused expression. She laughingly admitted that she wasn't used to showing up in "this format" and that she was having difficulty keeping her hovering above the floor to a minimum. She was just an inch or two off the ground, almost giggling as she floated upward. I gently pulled her down and steadied her until she adjusted. Newbies . . . I tell ya.

The ancient Egyptians depicted ghosts fully clothed, and that's how I see them too. Some people think it ridiculous that spirits should care about clothes, but I'm glad they do. For one thing, it would be pretty distracting to feel like I was in a nudist colony! I might be so busy trying to look everywhere else that I would miss the message. But more importantly, if the spirit is a stranger to me, their clothing helps me identify who they are and where and when they're from. It tells me about their age when they passed. The state of their clothes gives me clues about the circumstances of their death. For instance, Debbie's T-shirt and jeans told me she was relatively young. They were soaking wet, so I knew that she had most likely drowned. Clothes can be part of the message that ghosts or spirits are trying to convey, or a part of the spirit's self-image—an expression of how they remember themselves. It's all part of the message.

Not all spirit appearances are meant to convey a message. When the passing of a soul is near, when death approaches, occasionally there is a gathering of ghosts nearby, waiting to bring the journeying spirit to the new reality. Many have seen these presences hovering near a deathbed. A welcoming committee waiting for the soul that is near crossing is to be welcomed. It is a joyous gathering, and the lucky person who has one by his or her side will have a peaceful journey of passing.

Sometimes ghosts come to console us, to reassure loved ones of their continued existence and safety. A ghost that stands quietly in the corner may just be visiting to remember the love and tenderness that it experienced in the room. The presence of such a ghost brings a blessing to a gathering.

I believe that a ghost attending the conclusion of its incarnation—the ceremonial leave-taking and interment of its body—is not uncommon. It's a way for the spirit to say its adieus to earth and all those who have come together on its behalf for the funeral. The spirit may show up at the gathering in unexpected ways, such as in the form of an animal or object that friends and relatives associate with the departed. People who had a strong sense of humor in life will often display it again in their ghostly communications.

Lynn had a lot to tell me about the amusing and playful messages of ghosts. Lynn loved ladybugs—her house was always filled with them, and her fascination with them was a big joke among all her friends. "Just suck up the little suckers," she used to say as she handed me the vacuum cleaner, but we could all tell she loved them. As a friend and I were leaving the church on the day of Lynn's funeral, we saw a tiny ladybug on the door. We just looked at each other—we knew it was Lynn having fun with us.

Lynn wasn't shy about giving me practical advice from the other side, either. One day soon after she had crossed over, I was shopping for a running crop-top. I had one in my hand when Lynn's voice came through. "You don't need that," she said. I proceeded to have a silent conversation back and forth with her. "Yes, I do," I said, only to be answered with Lynn's firm "No, you don't." I decided to take her advice and left the store empty-handed, still grumbling a bit. Later, at home, I went through boxes of her clothes, trying to decide what to do with them. Among them I found a number of tops like the ones I had been shopping for. They fit me perfectly, and I had to laugh. Shopping advice was the last thing I would have expected from the spirit world.

The mechanics of communication are naturally different once we are in another dimension. Spirits often find it very difficult to communicate with the denser physical plane from their astral reality. They operate on a different frequency, where time and space have no meaning and communication is telepathic. As spirits and ghosts try to communicate with the living, they often have some difficulty playing by the rules of the physical world.

Spirits who are unaware that they've shed their physical body will initially attempt to communicate in the same ways they used to while they were incarnate, and they can get pretty inventive about it. They might hand me a note or a map, or offer symbolic representations that they hope I'll understand. They'll even play music that they sense has meaning to me. I especially enjoyed the ghost who played the *Close Encounters* ditty to get my attention. Now there was a spirit with a sense of humor!

It's often easier for people who were close to me in life to get through to me than those I didn't know. Their communications are stronger, and they don't need to resort to odd methods to reach me. The hints and clues of the message may be familiar, so they don't need so much translation on my part, either. If they want to let me know that they're around, they can do it in a number of ways, like showing up as a ladybug. They might generate a perfume or scent that I recognize as theirs, or place objects I associated with them in my path.

Swirls of color are another means for ghosts to say hello. Some of my loved ones have appeared to me as clouds of color, like tiny glints of light playing on the snow. One delightful visit came from a friend who, in life, was a small sprite of a woman. She appeared to me as a pixie, with sparkly dust-motes dancing all around her. "How do you like my new digs?" she said. Her husband looked down when I told him, the memory of his dear wife swelling his heart. My description of her visit was so like her—playful and fun. Other spirits have visited me as orbs, with colored rings of light expanding out from their bodies. The light show is always accompanied by a distinct essence that reflects the character I knew on Earth. Or they might materialize just as they were in life, but working within a slightly different set of rules.

Not long after Lynn passed, she came back to visit me in dreamtime. I was walking through a room, and she appeared in front of me in as solid a form as she embodied in waking reality. This surprised me. It is very unusual for a spirit to come back in solid form. "I'm dreaming," I said. "I know you're just an image. Why are you appearing like this to me? I know you're now ethereal, so why appear solid?"

She didn't answer, and wouldn't budge. She planted herself right in front of me, matching my every move as I shifted right and left in an attempt to move around her and continue my walk.

"Never mind why," she said. "Just dig deep and feel."

As soon as I began to really think about her, I became painfully aware of how much I *missed* Lynn. As soon as the pain of her absence hit me, I reached out to enfold her in my arms. This wasn't like any previous interaction I'd ever experienced between waking and dreaming. I could feel her physicality—her substance, volume, and weight. "How is this possible?" I said. "It doesn't make sense." Again, she told me to stop trying to rationalize and allow myself to feel.

The difference between my memory of her as she faded into the next life and how I experienced her presence in this dream was astonishing. Neither wavering nor unsteady, she stood tall. Her skin was smooth and healthy, her eyes bright and sparkling. Her hair shone, and gone was the wispiness I remembered from the chemotherapy. It felt so good just to hug her, hold her tight—to feel her vigor and health. I kept telling her how much I missed her.

After the heart-greeting, she sat down by a computer that appeared in the room. She began typing away, explaining how badly she wanted to communicate with people, but how cumbersome it was. I could see the determination in her eyes as she ran her fingers over the keyboard.

It was so like Lynn to use a computer in her attempts to communicate. In life, she had been interested in all things electronic. On the day she crossed, she let me know in her inimitable style that she was about to leave: she blew up the computer at her house and played havoc with the lights in mine, causing them to flicker on and off in every room I entered. In one particularly creative stroke, she sent me a message by fooling with my CD player while I was jogging. The CD kept skipping around, and I heard snippets from various songs that formed a message. "Time to say goodbye," the message began and went on from there.

> Today is the last day that I'm using words.
> They've gone now, lost their meaning, don't function anymore.
> I'm traveling, leaving logic and meaning.
> I'm traveling to the arms of unconsciousness.
> There's no greater power than the power of goodbye.
> Learn to say goodbye.
> I yearn to say goodbye.

I still get chills when I think about it or hear the music that played that day. I knew that she was flickering between the worlds. I stopped my jog and ran home, but I wasn't able to get to her before she died. Maybe she knew that would happen and chose to say goodbye to me in her own way.

Communication is, of course, a two-way street. Half of it depends on my ability to translate the particular "language" of the spirit. With luck I'm able to pick up on, decipher, and put together a message in a way that makes sense.

Ghosts' individual creative abilities as communicators make a big difference as to whether or not I can get their messages. Those who are better at communicating realize that it's far more effective using *my* associations to get an idea across rather then expecting me to understand *theirs*.

For instance, some ghosts realize that if they put their message in the context of a movie that I'm familiar with (since I'm a film junkie), I'll understand the meaning. Once, a spirit came into my dream as Kurt Russell. It took me a while to figure this one out, but I finally realized that the spirit was telepathically reading my associations not with Kurt Russell himself but with a role Kurt had played as a teacher in one of his films.

If the meaning of a message isn't clear at first, I ask for more detail and we try again. Spirits do their best to clarify, and I do my best to pick up on the cues. It's like a weird game of charades. Paying attention to synchronicities is often the key. It's all part of the art of allowing the communication to unfold in its own way and knowing that it may not all happen at once.

Many spirits prefer to come to us in the dreamtime. It's easier for them to do that because they know that we've let go of the logic we possess in the waking world. Dreaming reality is the realm of the ethereal, where spirits can meet each other whether they still have a life on the physical plane (like you and I) or live entirely on other planes. And so we have to pay attention to the encounters we have in dreamtime. When an ancestor or a loved one or an acquaintance comes to me in a dream, I do not doubt their reality or the reality of the visit. As far as I'm concerned, the meeting took place.

Occasionally someone will come to me in a dream with a message to convey to someone else. That was the case shortly after a great-aunt of mine had died. Her daughter, a registered nurse, had committed her life to looking after her mother for a number of years. My aunt wanted me to thank the daughter and tell her that she appreciated all that her daughter had done. "I know what she sacrificed for me," she said. "I want her to know that." For some reason, it's often hard for people to express love and gratitude, even when they feel it and know that it's there. Maybe they think it's a sign of sentimentality, a weakness of some kind. But really it is the strongest force on Earth, and the love we give to others makes a difference, whether we give it in big ways or in small ways. By relaying the message, I helped my aunt to express the gratitude that she must have felt she neglected to do in life. The daughter needed to know that her contribution was recognized, and both were healed in the process.

Healing the soul is more important than healing the body. This was brought home to me when I was with Lynn in her last days. She had, in the course of her life, repressed important parts of herself—the same psychic experiences and awareness that I had struggled with for so long. Now many of those parts were re-emerging. As we talked of our early friendship and the many extraordinary experiences we had together, she told me that she wanted me to know how important it was to be myself, no matter how odd it seemed to others. I needed to hear that, because at the time I was still harboring so many doubts about myself. Her words gave me the courage to be myself without fear.

Lynn also told me that she was back in touch with her spirit guide, and that he had brought her a vision. She saw clouds passing across the sky, displaying scenes from her life. It's pretty common for people who know the end is near to look back over their lives, but not usually in so graphic a manner. Lynn's description sounded like the kind of life review that many people who have had near death experiences report. They say that every detail of their life unfolds in front of them in a three-dimensional panorama, and they are able to see everything they have done, how their every action and thought affected those around them. The life review is a kind of judgment, but it is not God, they say, who is the judge: We judge ourselves. This is interesting because it means that our souls already know what is right or wrong. The people who come back from this life review also say that the near death experience changes the way they look at life. They truly understand the power of their free choice. They come to realize that love is more important than anything else.

Debbie the Flacker wanted something small—a moment of acknowledgment. A simple "Hello, I see you" isn't hard, but it was so important to her that she made a ghostly appearance to get it before she moved on. I still don't know who she was or what had happened to her. I'm just glad I was able to help. If you see a ghost, remember Douglas Adams' advice from *The Hitchhiker's Guide to the Galaxy:* don't panic! A simple "hello" will do.

CHAPTER 4

THE GREYS

journal entry
Wednesday, January 14, 2003

It wasn't so bad at first, when it was like the crunching of dry autumn leaves underfoot. But still, a small chill ran up my spine and down the backs of my legs like a breeze from the long shadows of approaching winter. It felt like a warning of the cold.

As I listened, the sound grew. What is that? I thought. Is that leaves? No, not leaves. It was too persistent, too relentless. It was something in the walls, something that wanted to come out. It was more of a . . . scuttling. Like a swarm of a thousand insects coming out of the walls, perhaps, coming from nowhere and everywhere.

Images flitted through my mind—the dust bowl, the trembling farmer, Egypt, locusts with mandibles clicking in voracious appetite.

The hairs down the back of my neck stood on end. I felt a nameless dread. Then I saw them—the source of my growing fear. Grey figures—looming, needy, hungry, wanting. They were huddled together, bound to each other by their dark energies, by the heaviness of their woe. They clothed themselves in this woe, gathering it around themselves for whatever ragged warmth it might provide. But of course there was no warmth. There was only poverty, cold, rejection, and aching, desperate hunger.

They surged towards me in a mass, wanting. Wanting what? Nothing, everything. Just wanting, empty, filled with lack. Huge with lack.

All of a sudden, I felt tiny—a small light in the oppressive despair that moved toward me. If that darkness reached me, I would be lost, consumed, left as nothing but a stalk stripped of its grain.

My mind hurried to build the box of mirrors that would protect me. Above, below, forward, and back, the reflective surfaces began to take shape, but it was too late. Already I could feel the dark energy starting to suck me under.

"Ooooh, #%&*!!!" I thought. "Get me outta here!" And with that I was gone.

Like the song says, know when to hold 'em, know when to fold 'em, know when to walk away. Or in this case, run. I woke up feeling like I had barely been able to free myself from a horde of drowning souls grabbing onto me in an attempt to save themselves. One more millisecond, and I would have been dragged down with them.

I went over the encounter again and again. I recalled a brief moment before I ran when I noticed one soul slightly set apart from the others. I had thought that if I could just separate her from the rest, I could point her to the light. But she was so self-absorbed, so involved in her own pain, that I couldn't penetrate her crushing, bleak emptiness. Maybe she didn't want to change—she only wanted to draw me into her own misery. If I had met her when she was alone, I would have done more, but as it was she had been too close to the force of the collective, and there had been no time. I felt like a youth worker who sees the possibility of helping a girl on the fringe of a gang. If you can get her alone, you may be able to talk to her, but it's not possible while the others are around.

Souls with similar vibrations clump together like magnets and create an energy that is far stronger than that of the individual souls that form the collective. It's the same force that creates a mob mentality. Individuals can be caught up and pulled into the undertow of dark energies. It's very hard to reach these souls, but eternity is a long time and eventually the lightworkers are able to draw them out, one by one.

The Greys, unable to sense the light, exist in a hell of their own making. Places like purgatory or hell are not actual places; they're only two of the infinitely possible mental residences we design and live in. We construct them for ourselves with our thoughts, our daydreams, and the emotions our daydreams generate.

Thoughts chatter through our minds in every waking moment. They become so much like traffic noise that we cease to notice them. By the time we're adults, we've formed beliefs—personal truths that we've accepted wholeheartedly and don't bother to look at anymore. We wear them like comfortable old slippers. But sometimes our slippers get so old we have to get a new pair, and sometimes our personal truths have to change because they're not working anymore. We suffer, become ill, or sink into misery. Then we need to look at our beliefs, take stock of our daydreams.

Thoughts and daydreams are prayers offered up and answered at every turn. Source answers them without judgment. Many of us have favorite sayings that we use to express our beliefs. We might say over and over, "I just can't make ends meet," or "It's a dog-eat-dog world," unaware that these continual litanies shape our experience. If we think of thoughts as prayers, we will look at them in a different way. Do we really want to pray that ends will never meet, or that people are only out for themselves?

Your prayer thoughts are important. They are as important as the contemplations of God. When you pray to your god, to Source, you also pray to yourself. That is because you are Source and Source is you. So take care. Be aware of what you think. Do not dismiss your imaginings as unimportant in the larger scheme of things. Your soul's energy, created by thoughts and feelings, reverberates throughout the universe, into other dimensions, and beyond the brief time you spend here on Earth. Much as we would like to think that our thoughts and emotions are completely self-contained, it isn't that easy. We can be lifted by the happiness of a friend, or brought low by the anger or depression of another. Your interior and exterior worlds affect mine. Our minds and bodies are in constant communication with our mental and physical surroundings. We are both transmitters and receivers of the energy frequencies of intent and emotion.

We need to pay attention.

Emotions are scripted by thoughts. The images and stories we create to illustrate our thoughts make an interior world that is then projected out into material reality. When we drift into the theater of our thoughts, these thoughts take us to an emotional place. We get swept up in the emotions the play or the movie that we've made evokes in us. We've hypnotized ourselves and we act on our own hypnotic suggestions.

This is not a one-person show, and that's what makes it interesting. We are the author of our part in the play but our part is only one of many. We get to write our character as we go along, moment by moment, developing him or her any way we wish. We write our own dialogue.

Imagine that your life is a soap opera, and that in watching it each day, you're thrilled by the melodrama that you construct on the screen of your mind. Sometimes emotions are like that, like the delicious tawdriness of melodrama. Sometimes we *like* to wallow in the rich fabrications of sorrow and grand tragedy because they make engaging stories and generate lurid and lively conversations. But when we get caught up, when we forget that it is a soap opera, it is not so much fun. It seems that the story is real, and indeed it is, because we've made it so.

Dark imaginings and black thoughts can be very seductive. Some people create gloomy castles of darkness, build torture chambers into them, and then hunker down in the dungeon because it is such a luscious gothic image, given romantic cachet by literature and films. These people dress in dark clothing and ponder their alienation. They call anyone who points to all the beautiful light and love evident in the world naïve and unrealistic.

Many people reinforce their worldview by looking around and choosing to see only what confirms it—and lord knows there's a lot of food out there for their mental mandibles to munch on: the violence that passes as entertainment, the scary news reports of endless war, racial hatred, murder, and greed. The list could go on and on. Some people come to see all this sorrow and pain not as part of life, but as life itself. They like to say that "life is a vale of tears," because it's a handy quote that confirms a limited perception of the human experience. As they walk the sad paths they are carving in the landscape of their thoughts, depression and despair cloud their brains like a thick fog that shuts out light and isolates them from fellow travelers. They sink into the dark quagmire of their own emotions until there seems to be no escape from it. No matter how much they struggle, they are pulled ever deeper into the dense, heavy emotions their thoughts are creating. They have stepped into the quicksand of sorrow.

Like the Greys, these people can become desperate for light, desperate for some sense of love, forgetting that if they want to find light and love they need to find it in themselves. The Greys have forgotten how to love themselves, too. They think love is something that comes from outside of themselves, that God has abandoned them. They have forgotten that they are one with Source and that it is they who turned away from their light.

To someone caught in the grip of their sorrow, hopelessness, and disempowerment, suicide may seem the only way out, but it isn't. The same thoughts and emotions that lead to suicide will be carried to the other side because they come from within. There is no way for a soul to escape itself.

You are not responsible for the world, but you are responsible for yourself, and the interior worlds that you make. The good news is that we are not slaves to our emotions, although at times it may seem so. Ask any teenager. We say, "I feel this way, and this is the way I feel. I can't help it!" But we can help it. And sometimes we must help it or be consumed by it. If we're lost and frightened in the dark, we need to cast light into the shadows. We need to look at thoughts and emotions in a different way if we want to change their shape.

We can look at emotion as a form of energy that has vibrational frequency. In the dreamtime, I experience this frequency as a number of combined qualities: sound, color, degrees of heaviness and buoyancy, light and dark, physical sensations—abrasiveness or silkiness or prickliness. This may seem like an unusual concept, but consider: we say someone is in a red rage or a black mood or a blue funk or a grey depression or is green with envy. Emotions have color. Joy trills like a merry flute; sorrow has the mournful timbre of the cello. Emotions have sound. We can feel low or high. A cold chill of fear can run through us, or a warm surge of love. These elements of color, sound, temperature, and so on combine to create unique chords—the particular frequency of the emotion.

Therapists can use one element—color or sound or scent—to alter the general tenor of an emotion, as like affects like. If we expose ourselves to a particular color frequency during the course of therapy, the effect does not disappear when the color is turned off. That's because the color of the emotion itself has changed. The same goes for sound. If we alter one quality of an emotion, we affect its entirety.

We don't necessarily need therapists to use this principle. We can bathe ourselves mentally in a color associated with a frequency, or imagine a sound that resonates with it, and as we do, we evoke the emotion belonging to that frequency.

Imagine also that emotions are in a spectrum, with each emotion having a counterpart somewhere along the spectrum. Hatred at the low end is counterbalanced by love at the high end. Each heavy vibration can be lifted by its counterpart—envy by gratitude, jealousy by generosity, depression by joy, and despair by hope. Imagine that the spectrum does not go up and down like a ladder, but side-to-side like a piano keyboard. Emotions become like musical instruments that we can master over time.

Emotions of similar frequency tend to bond inside an individual—love, forgiveness, and gratitude form a group, as do hate, revenge, and complaint. If we foster any one of the emotions that belong to a frequency range, we automatically activate the others on that part of the scale. If we practice forgiveness, we nurture and enhance the gratitude that is allied with it. It doesn't matter where we start. All paths lead to Rome.

Particular emotions can carry both positive and negative poles. Anger can be a positive thing, for instance, if it liberates someone from the apathetic acceptance of abuse, if it turns a person back toward self-love. Sometimes an angry fight can clear the air between individuals, or open up avenues of honesty and understanding that weren't there before. Relatively speaking, then, anger in some circumstances is cleansing, like a summer rainstorm after a long dry spell. On the other hand, anger can manifest as a negative persistent sullenness that eats away at joy. Sometimes darkness can be a velvety cocoon, a place of private contemplation, or a frightening gloom. And sometimes the sun is blessedly warming, while at others its rays are relentless and punishing. In other words, positive or negative aspects of emotions are relative to their effects—whether they are taking us closer to or further away from the vibration of love, the vibration of our higher selves, or the resonant frequencies of Source.

We can utilize tools to influence our emotions, then. We don't need to act as if we are their victims. People sometimes say if there is a god, how can he let all the suffering in the world happen? Why does he let us suffer? How can we answer such questions?

We are not puppets dancing on a set of strings that God manipulates. That's not how it works. Such questions spring from a sense of helplessness, from our perception that people are victims of forces beyond their control. They assume the separation of God from human existence and deny our co-creation with Source.

Sometimes there *are* forces beyond our control—natural disasters, for instance, or the death of a loved one. It's how we interpret and respond to these events that brings us misery or joy. We aren't forced to simply allow pain or rage to have their way with us; if we look within, we can see that it is our responses that shine the light on the author of our emotions. Circumstances don't define us, they reveal us.

There are also many circumstances that we can, as individuals and societies, control. We should not ask how God could let all the woes of the world happen, but how *we,* in our divinity, could let them happen. God does not wage war or let children starve. We do that. The question—how could God let this happen?—seeks to blame someone or something else. When we ask it, we relinquish our power and deny the choices we have made as divine incarnations.

Part of the contract of incarnating as human is the understanding that we have free will, or intent. I recall a dream in which I consciously chose and directed all my will toward love. We can choose what emotions and actions to harbor. We can form the intention to love by using our will, our choice, to act with love. Before we act, we can ask ourselves, "What would I do if I were the embodiment of love?" and, "Given the choice, would I rather be kind or be right?" Which do you think would create a better world?

Let's consider some other questions. How can we return to the garden of our innocent and pure love, the one we thought we left behind when we fell into flesh? And why was flesh a falling? Why is it that the material world is considered a falling, a separation from the sacred? What if there was no fall and we never left the garden? What if it is all around us and in us?

I believe that it is. Until we learn to respect the material world and ourselves as the divine embodiment of God, we will not cease suffering. When we consider physical being as evil, as separated from God, we punish ourselves and the Earth upon which we live. We make ourselves suffer not for something we did, but for what we are and, while we are in incarnation, what we cannot help being.

At first, the Greys seemed like evil beings sunk in the darkness. But they weren't evil, any more than you are when you suffer. Good and evil are words of separation and moral judgment. In my work in the dreamtime, I need to be free of judgment because compassion—the greatest tool of healing—thrives in acceptance of difference. I need to find what I have in common with another soul so that I can communicate and empathize.

I'm not sure why we humans think certain emotions are occasions for guilt. Guilt only makes things worse. I've had the experience of looking at someone and making an unkind judgment, then berating myself for that judgment, and then further berating myself for berating myself. If I hadn't realized where I was going, I could have ended up beating myself up and then wondering why I felt so dreadful for days afterward.

We all want happy and fulfilled lives. We want to be perfect—perfectly good or happy or loving. But perfectionism is a harsh taskmaster—the truth is that we have human flaws and we all stumble—and stuffing down unpleasant thoughts and emotions turns us away from self-love. Our desire to be good can become a rod of punishment that pulls us farther from God than ever. No good comes of self-hatred or wallowing in shame. All the benevolence that we direct at others must also be directed inward, toward ourselves. That way, we can truly feel it and share it. The paradox of emotion is that the more of one you give away—whether love/forgiveness or hatred/revenge—the more of it you get back.

We come to Earth to enrich our souls with material experience, to learn the hard lessons, and always to bring incarnation into closer alliance with the will of our higher selves and our participation in the endless creation of Source. As we do this with our thoughts and intentions, prompted by the comfort or disease of our emotions, we learn to juggle the eternal interplay between the light and the dark. We learn the skills of protection from forces we don't want to harbor and openness to those we do.

We can put unwanted thoughts aside. We don't have to take them out to lunch and entertain them. Worrying over negative thoughts only gives them strength and by worrying, we give energy and power to the source of the thought. If we feel an emotion intruding on us, we can use powerful tools of visualization and guided meditation to keep it out. Following are some of my mental tools. You're welcome to use them if they resonate with your set of beliefs, but of course they are not the only methods around. You can make up your own prayers and evocations, using names and images that are most comfortable to you.

Whenever you feel the oppressive weight of unwanted dark energy, surround yourself in white light. There's a multitude of ways to visualize this: imagine being showered or cocooned in white light, or for even deeper tangible connection, imagine light from the sun shining down on you, entering through the top of your head and cascading like a river of golden honey throughout your body before finally exiting through your feet.

Simultaneously **ground yourself.** Imagine your feet growing roots that plunge deep into the Earth, anchoring you firmly to this planet. You are grounded and open to Source energy. Say, "All that is not mine, please leave." If you feel you need more help, you can also call in angels of protection.

For self-protection, visualize setting up two-way mirrors all around you as if you're in a box. Say, "Creator, fill me and surround me with white and gold light of protection so that only love may enter and only love can go out." Ask for any negativity to be burned up in the light. All unwanted energies are reflected back immediately to the source they came from and are burned up in the light.

In a situation where you encounter an unknown energy (as in perhaps a "ghostly" encounter), ask if the entity you've met is from the light. If it's not, send it away. On the other hand, if it is a confused soul, offer empathy.

Tell it that it has crossed over and it's now time to go into the light.

If you enter a "cold" room and feel the energy there is dark, ground yourself. Call in your guides, masters, teachers, and healers of the light. It's very important to always call in beings "from the light." You don't want to have just anyone show up, as that can potentially invite disaster. Ask that the "gateway" be closed to any dark energies and dark forces forever. Then ask for angels of protection to stay there permanently.

When you're feeling fear, remember that you can only feel one emotion at a time. Quickly replace the negative emotion of fear with love. You can do this by thinking of something that brings you joy, like holding a smiling baby, feeling a warm spring breeze, playing with a puppy, or whatever joy looks like to you. Surround yourself in light. Breathe into your heart chakra. If you don't breathe during a potentially traumatic situation, you may "hold" the trauma in the cells of a particular part of your body, and you'll then need to work on releasing that trauma at some point. It's much easier to get into the practice of breathing. Focus on shooting love toward the source of fear from your heart chakra.

As we learn to use tools of protection, we grow resilient and strong. Knowing that our emotional integrity is safe, we can afford to be open, receptive, and generous with our love. If we are ill, we can begin to heal, as long as we trust what our body is trying to tell us.

Doctors know that hormonal and chemical changes accompany changes in emotion. Medical intuitives are often able to make connections between emotions held in the body that are specific to an incident in the patient's past life and certain illnesses or diseases. Journey work—delving through meditation and trance into the relationship between body and soul—reveals experiences from our other lives that revisit us, through the body, in this life.

Bodies, then, hold the memories of lifetimes of thought and emotion and belief in their very cells. Emotions may seem like they have no substance, but they are reflected in the body.

Imagine that someone you are in a relationship with abuses you. You are filled with rage and humiliation. The situation becomes intolerable, and you decide to leave the relationship. You walk away, and refuse to speak to your abuser any more. What has happened to your rage? Every time you think of your abuser, it wells up again, and it still feels awful. You may have left the abusive situation, but the feelings associated with it are still residing within you. Part of you is being held hostage to your past.

Walking away from a negative situation does not free you from the past if you carry your rage about it like a talisman of suffering. While you chew away on your rage, it also gnaws away at you. In the same way, guilt, hatred, or thirst for revenge can eat away at you in a very real way—as physical disease.

To avoid this, it is important that we dig up those painful memories and find a way to transform them. During the course of our journey work, we take back the power we have given to chemicals or surgeries or the idea that we play no part in our illness and its healing.

Acknowledging a destructive emotion is the beginning of healing. Once you take this step, you can ask yourself why you feel the way you do and how you can change it. By being honest with yourself, you can initiate an open conversation exploring your emotions, your body, and the ways they affect each other.

We don't need to cage up unwanted emotions like dangerous beasts. We only need to gently guide them, like loving parents, and be patient and wise with ourselves. To forgive others—to heal the ruptures in our relationships—we must first forgive ourselves, and love ourselves. This is not always easy to do. We become accustomed to the internal monologue that tells us that whatever we do, it is not enough, that our small gestures of kindness can do nothing to change the world. Knowing that this is not true is the first step towards empowerment.

Our higher self does not get caught up in the turmoil that our emotions create in our conscious mind. It watches from the wings like a theatrical director, assessing the unfolding plot and character development. It makes suggestions about the best ways to fulfill the chart—the script we wrote before coming here. If it notices that certain emotions and the actions that arise from them do not further the plot, it suggests changes that might make things work better. We should listen to this higher self—if we act like renegades on the stage who will heed neither playwright nor director, the play will go drastically wrong. Sometimes the director has to be firm, throw a fit, even introduce catastrophe or illness. He has to force us to listen.

Trust your inner voice. It knows you best. Listen, however softly your higher self speaks. Do not make it scream to make itself heard. Don't let its voice be drowned out by the booming of those around you—authorities and teachers and traditions and the media. Don't let its gentle directions become lost in the cacophony of voices telling you what is right, what to do, how to think.

Learn to remember the language of your higher self. The signs and guides are all around us, right here in the material world, in inspirations, synchronicities, and dreams. You were born with innate knowledge of the language of your higher self. You were born speaking the subtle language of your soul.

The purpose of life is not to get away from it. Life is not a vale of tears or a veil of fears. It is much more—a magnificent display of creation. Let us treat it as such and give it the respect it deserves. Life is a gift we have given ourselves.

When someone else gives us a present, we know it is simply good manners to thank them, to appreciate the effort made to pick it up, wrap it, and deliver it. Let us give our soul the same credit. We did not come here to punish ourselves. We came here to grow in the lush exuberance of earthly experience. And believe it or not, we also came here to have a good time. Imagine that!

The joyless Greys missed the boat on having a good time, but not forever. They'll get another chance to lighten up. In every darkness, no matter how large, there is a spark of light. May they find the spark of their joy again and find their way home to the welcoming arms of love and Source. Even to them the universe will say Namaste—the divine in me greets the divine in you. Your spirit and mine are one. But man! Did you ever take the long way home!

CHAPTER 5

THE HEALING

journaL entry
Friday, November 1, 2002
This is the first time I've knowingly worked with a team of energy healers.

I have been astrally "dropped" into something already in progress and for a moment I'm unsure where I am or what is happening. As I try to orient myself, I notice a young man asleep and floating horizontally above a bed. We are not alone for long. Seven figures gather around him. They are intent, filled with purpose.

These figures are ethereal light beings. A brilliant glow emanates from their heart centers. Even though I perceive them as light, I can vaguely see that they wear robes that fall to their feet as they float in the matrix.

We are surrounded by darkness. I have no sense of geometric boundary. There is no top or bottom, no constraining side walls in the space of our healing.

The figures don't touch or speak to each other as they line up on either side of the patient, four on his right side and three on his left. I move into the space remaining, bringing our number to eight.

Now I know what to do. I've done this before. We have assembled here to heal this young man. There is no communication or instruction; we all know our parts. Together we proceed to work in a seamless choreography to cleanse, eradicate, release, and clear the man's physical body of disease. Our efforts are utterly synchronized in the knowing that only together is it possible for us to draw the diseased energy out.

We don't touch him. I watch as our collective energies merge, twining together to create a vortex which rises up, taking with it all the clinging, unclean elements and dispersing them above the man's body.

I don't know if this young man was aware of the astral bodies working on him. Considering he was asleep at the time, I doubt it. It's possible that he registered the events as his own dream; perhaps when he awakened he experienced a wonderful warmth and a sense of love coursing through his body without knowing why. I can't say for sure.

In my dream, the lightworkers' heart centers glowed brighter than the sun. The iridescent pigments I used in my paintings only hint at the shimmering and shifting light emanating from their hearts. My intent was to illustrate that they vibrate at a lighter, higher frequency, and the highest frequency is love—so I chose white and yellow to depict the intense love I felt from them.

The dark, heavy blue-grey color I used for the man being healed reflects his low and depressive state of being. He is depicted with the interior shapes of muscle and organ exposed to indicate how I'm able to look into a body when I'm in the Knowing.

The abstract, rectangular shapes in the background suggest the various layers of reality that need to be traversed in order to reach a patient on a non-material plane. Each layer is slightly transparent and laid one upon the other in a visual description of the depths and dimensions that exist simultaneously in the fabric of the matrix.

I've used the term "the Knowing" to describe the feeling I sense in the dreamtime. In the Knowing, all necessary information is instantly available. It is similar to intuition—the faculty of sensing something without using the linear processes of the logical mind. The Knowing is complete immersion in the realm of intuition. Healing in the Knowing—part of what I do on the Night Shift—occurs in the astral plane.

Energy healing has been practiced by many cultures for thousands of years. The force used to heal is known in India as *prana,* in China as *qi.* The Japanese practice *reiki;* in Hebrew energy is called *ruah;* in Hawaii it is referred to as *mana* or *ti.* Acupuncture and acupressure, which use knowledge of energy flow in the physical body, have recently gained widespread acceptance in the Western world. Therapeutic touch, the laying on of hands, healing prayer, and faith healing all have long traditions as well.

These practices can be learned, suggesting that most people have a capacity for healing that goes beyond the physically-oriented approach of Western allopathic medicine. Even as the ideas and practices of energy work gain wider acceptance in the West, many doctors are reluctant to incorporate it into their practices. Their view of the human body as machine discounts the roles that belief and intent play in the generation of disease.

Growing up, I knew nothing of alternative medicine or the venerable traditions of other cultures. And yet I used the very energies and forces that are only now gaining acceptance in the West. So how did I learn?

Healing is innate to my being. It comes as naturally to me as the bear's urge to hibernate in the winter. The bear doesn't sit and ponder the origin or purpose of his instinct as winter draws near, nor does he go to Hibernation School to learn how it's done. He just knows. It was the same with me.

As a child, I never thought twice about using the power of energy to heal. When I was awake and saw someone who needed help, I would reach out instinctively to lay my hands on or near him or her, allowing what came naturally to move through me, wanting only to help. I knew intuitively how to use intent and focus to let love flow through me into the person in need. I didn't hesitate to let my intuition guide me, nor did I question my ability to direct energy in this way. My childhood healings drew on memories from the in-between, where energy is the coin of exchange.

At that stage, the fantastic worlds of superhero comic books and science fiction came closer to my reality than anything else I read or was taught. Like the superheroes, I felt I was different, that I possessed a secret. Naturally, I came to love characters like Spiderman because I identified with them and the powers they possessed.

Of course, even as a child I knew my abilities to manipulate energy were not "superhero powers," and I'm glad, too—I think I would have looked ridiculous in tights. I knew that I had been given a gift that I was meant to use in the service of others. I sensed that my gifts were given to me from some force that worked through me.

Things changed as I grew older. I came to learn, as all people do, the rules and regulations of the society in which I live and what is counted as "real" by most people in my culture. As I began to understand that my innate perceptions were not shared by my family, my peers, or my religious community, I became plagued by doubts. What if my experiences weren't real? What if they came from some less-than-wholesome source? They were so strong and persistent that I could not discount them, yet I did come for a while to doubt their *meaning*.

I tried to find the answers, but I wasn't sure where to look. By the time I got to high school, there were only a couple of friends I could talk to, and they didn't know any more than I did. The library had nothing. The Internet didn't exist yet. I tried once to reach out to a private group of psychics who got together once a month for meditations. They told me that they couldn't help me because my energy outpaced the group collectively. It was beyond their experience. That was a sad, lonely, frightening day!

My questions left unanswered, I became afraid that I might mistakenly do more harm than good—not only to others, but also to myself. This worry was brought home one day when I was at a sleepover with my best friend. She went upstairs after dinner and when I followed her minutes later, I found her curled up on the floor in a tight ball of pain. Someone I loved was hurting. All other thoughts fled from my mind. My only question was, "Where does it hurt?" She pointed to her stomach and gasped out that she thought she had food poisoning. I asked her to lie flat on her back, close her eyes, and focus on where it hurt. Eyes closed, I concentrated completely on taking her pain away. That was the only thought in my mind—I gave myself utterly to it.

Later, my friend said, "I felt a localized heat over my belly. It got progressively hotter and hotter, until it was almost burning. I was so curious that I had to peek, and I saw Monica kneeling by my side. She had her eyes closed and her hands hovered about six inches above my stomach. I closed my eyes again and then felt the strange sensation of a hand passing through my skin. I could literally feel her fingers and palm as she reached into my belly—but it wasn't as though the skin or body had been breached in any way. It didn't hurt and there was no pressure, really. Just the totally real feeling of a hand moving right through my skin without any resistance. Once inside my body, it grabbed onto something and then retracted, pulling whatever it was out through the skin. The instant the invisible hand retreated with its prize, I felt better. The pain was gone just like that."

When I saw that my friend was better, I suddenly felt very ill myself. Nausea and weakness swept over me and I had to lie down. My friend was very upset, telling me that she never would have allowed me to heal her if she had known that I would absorb her pain. I was feeling too poorly to talk about it, but the fact that her pain had concentrated inside my body took me by surprise as much as it did her. At that time I was completely unaware that there are ways to release the energy drawn out during a healing. It was not until years later that I learned to draw, cleanse, and release energy so that it would pass through and beyond me.

After that incident, I avoided healing for many years—in the waking world, at least. Instead, I chose to work with energy primarily in the dreamtime, where questions and doubts fall away in the Knowing. I recall my dreams with as much clarity as others recall their waking life.

As I continue my research and studies on both sides of reality, I've come to accept astral worlds and the material world equally. They are both utterly real, interpenetrating each other and vibrating at different frequencies. But I will tell you this: In my experience, the other side or dreamtime or the matrix or whatever you want to call it is far more vibrant, alive, and intense than the linear, logical world of matter.

As an adult, I've come to understand that the work I do in the dreamtime comes from my participation in Source energy. Creation is not a single event, but an ongoing interaction with the energies that fuel life. We are not, as human beings, bystanders in the events that unfold around us. Source is as much in us as we are in it; we are conjoined in the dance of continual unfolding.

This didn't entirely sink in until I let go of the notion that I was separate from unified wholeness. My upbringing seemed to be one big lesson in separation. I grew up in a religious community that envisioned God as a creator sitting outside His own creation, judging—a God that separated our actions into good or evil and squabbled with other religions over His name. I grew up in a philosophical community that glorified intellect—the voice of objective authority—over intuition or inner knowing. Absorbing these values can separate us from ourselves, dismissing a vital part of our consciousness as delusion or fantasy.

In *my* reality, my intuition, knowledge, and nightly lived experience, we are loved, no matter what. And I can love without limit or condition, can share with Source unbounded love not just for a favored few, but for all that is, for all that we create together. We are one.

My reality has been that God is not separate from us. Source embraces us all. We are drops in the cosmic ocean that we call by the many names that religion and science have chosen to confer on wholeness. The ocean is not separate from its components, just as our own bodies are not separate from the cells and molecules and atoms that form our very flesh.

The ability to heal at the energy level does not depend on membership in any particular religion or school of philosophy. I have my own way of explaining it, personal expressions that resonate with me—but you may very well have your own framework in which to talk about the invisible worlds of spirit. You may not even believe in a spirit world, choosing instead to turn to science for your understanding of how energy works and what it can do. Quantum physics, for example, offers a language and model for understanding worlds of possibility brought into existence through thought.

It is my belief that human beings are capable of wonderful and miraculous things. Together with Source we can focus our intent to heal each other energetically, but certain conditions are necessary to create this. The simple act of intention to offer love, light, and healing is the core of the practice. When I set my intention, I also ask Source to make me a clear channel or conduit for all that is good to come through. Again, I do not think that I possess any godlike powers; I am merely a channel working in eternal union with higher energies.

So how does it work? I've talked about how as a child I knew instinctively what to do to create a state of energy healing. In a nutshell, I used a combination of **intent + focus** to produce **result.** Thinking about something brought me results. Even as a child I knew that my thoughts created my reality, and happily that rather huge concept is not a secret anymore!

Over time, I've made a few more distinctions in my understanding, and the healing equation looks a little more like this:

Intent + Love + Unconditional Giving + Focus = Positive Results.

This formula is simple. It doesn't require medical knowledge, just human compassion and the ability to concentrate and focus. As an adult, I've been able to bring my intuitive knowledge to personal medical studies in waking life—but I must stress that any information I receive and pass on should be checked out with a specialist from the medical community on this side. Any information that comes through from guides or channeling should absolutely be confirmed and clarified with medical practitioners here. The objective is teamwork.

While I'm fully aware that anything is possible in the dream state, one of my greatest challenges has been to accept the idea that not everyone I work with on the energy level will be healed, and that healing does not always mean cure. There are a number of reasons why this might be so.

We come into life with the intention to learn from our time on Earth. Individuals enter incarnation with a chart, or mission, and illness may just be part of someone's personal mission statement. On a soul level, difficulties offer a very valuable opportunity for growth. It is in the midst of adversity that we begin to ask questions—Why me? Why now? We can come to better know ourselves through challenging circumstances, for as we question our lives, we contemplate our part in shaping them. Who am I really? What do I want out of life? What do I believe deep in my heart? Sometimes people need hardship to encourage them to illuminate the dark and dusty corners that they have been neglecting.

At times, it's better to not heal someone. At a lecture one day, an older woman approached me after hearing that I was a healer. We became engaged in conversation, and she told me something of her life and beliefs and then began to describe her ailments. As soon as she did, I knew that was why she had come to speak to me. She wanted help. I was acutely aware that she wanted me to heal her. At the same time I felt very strongly that if I did, I would be doing her a disservice. She knew all about the power of thought and intent, but didn't yet believe that she could apply it to her life. She still hoped someone else would make the journey to responsibility for her—in effect ceding her will to another. Her desire to lean on someone was preventing her from claiming her own power.

I kept the conversation focused on what *she* could do, assuring her that I knew she had the power she needed within herself. I had draped my arm across the back of her chair and, unbeknownst to her, sent thoughts of love her way. I could see the light come on in her eyes as she finally got what I was saying: her journey was *self*-empowerment. For me to have healed her would only have reinforced her belief that her connection to Source lay somewhere outside herself.

Serious illness, then, can be a step on the road to greater understanding of the purpose of your life. That sounds like a tough one to swallow, but there it is. Your higher self may want you to have this earthly experience and it is not for me or anyone else to take it away from you. Illness and hardship can open doors to unexpected gifts of self-realization. It's all in what you choose to take from the experience.

The power of thought and belief plays a vital role in what happens in the course of healing. There must not be any doubt on the part of either the giver or the receiver that the body can be affected by the energy and positive intent of thought. Each moment in the process is an exercise in trust. If someone does not believe that healing by these means is possible, then they will reject its truth not only in their minds but also in their bodies. Again, that is their choice.

Healing, then, is permission-based. It can't be forced on an individual, just as love cannot be thrust on an unwilling recipient. If people have an emotional investment in their own illness, they may in fact not want to be healed, as odd as that sounds. I learned this in a dream in which I approached a woman in a wheelchair. At first I wondered if she was even alive. She was exuding a bluish gangrene from the inside out, as if a kind of rot was trying to push its way to the surface of her skin. I reached out to place my hand gently on her shoulder, but just as I was about to make contact, she broke out of her stillness to unleash an unbelievable wave of anger towards me. She called me by name, which was unusual and unsettling. "Who the hell do you think you are?" she yelled. "How dare you presume to touch me? What makes you think I want any of your damn healing?" Taken aback and much saddened, I drew away, feeling chastened and confused. I felt as though I had been slapped across the face.

Someone must have heard that thought. The next night, I was visited by a woman in the dreamtime. "We're sorry you were hit," she said, "but we all love you and we're here for you." I felt much comforted by her presence and her words. In the meantime, I had learned a valuable lesson.

Is healing in the astral plane, where my work on the Night Shift is carried out, the same as energy healing in the material plane? The answer is yes and no. I use energy while I am in my ethereal body, but I am operating in both the astral and the material planes. My healing, then, takes place in ethereal form. Sometimes the body I'm healing may be in its ethereal form when we meet in the dream-time. At other times, my ethereal form goes directly to a person's physical body.

The matrix encompasses both astral and material re-alities. Each has a different frequency, so that most peo-ple can't see ethereal bodies, which vibrate at a higher frequency, around them. Everyone has an ethereal body, however, and it travels in the dreamtime, just as mine does. This body resembles the physical body, but it is a mental construct, a form of energy held together by con-scious thought and intent.

When they hear that their ethereal body travels to as-tral realms in dreams, some people may worry that the physical body is left empty at those times, its soul departed to another place. This is not the case. Some say that the ethereal body is attached to the physical body by a silver cord, severed only at death. I've only seen that cord once, but at no time do I feel that I have vacated my physical self as I travel in other dimensions. Remember, many dreams are visits to the astral plane. You fall asleep at night secure that you will wake up in your body tomorrow. Your higher consciousness knows perfectly well that your soul will not be lost from your body. In a sense, the astral plane is not only part of the wider universe that embraces us, but also part of an inner universe. It is both in us and around us.

Healing in the dreamtime has a totally different quality than energy work in waking reality, though the results may be the same. In the Knowing, I feel a certainty and trust. I know exactly what to do. That's a good thing, too, because in the dreamtime, I have no time to ask questions. I am usually dropped into a situation with about .02 nanoseconds to figure out where I am, who I'm with, and what it is that they need. I call this "astral triage," which includes not only healing but also emergency rescue. I'm suddenly immersed in the necessity of the moment; there's no time for doubt or hesitation. If you imagine a paramedic arriving on the scene of an emergency, you'll have a good idea of what it's like. Emergency workers on both sides spring into action without taking time to sit around and think about it all. That's the nature of the job.

The reasons that I'm called vary; I never know until I arrive on the scene. I do know, however, that I'm able to respond to a call for help without the constraints of space or time. As soon as the need is felt, I'm there—even though my physical body may be miles away from the material body of the person in need. Each experience is different from the previous one—never a repeat performance.

If I were to write a manual on astral triage, I would definitely point out that what I do in the dreamtime makes a very real difference in the physical world. In addition to my healings, I manipulate or move objects, and send out strong mental suggestions. I came to this realization when I first saw people, places, and events on the news or in newspapers that were the same people, places, and events I saw during my astral flights.

Objects and people can be affected by what I call a *push thought*. I take all of the emotion within my entire being, bring it together in one big ball of emotional and mental energy, pull it to the surface, and then release it in a burst of ultimate focus on whatever it is I wish to create.

When I answer a call, I know that although I'm in my astral body—an ethereal state where time has no meaning—the same can't necessarily be said for those I'm helping who are tethered to their physical bodies. In their reality, there are sometimes situations where every second counts.

This came home to me one day several years ago. I had answered a call about an accident in which a bus full of children had careened into a river. The vehicle was quickly sinking into the rushing waters, its young passengers still trapped inside. I suddenly found myself underwater. Looking through the windows, I could see the panicking children inside, screaming. They were pressing their little hands against the windows and I could see the horror and fear in their eyes as two or three of them made eye contact with me. I sent them a huge push thought, encouraging them to go towards the emergency exit. The children rushed to the back of the bus and struggled to open the door, but their small muscles were no match for the pressure of the water holding it shut. I mustered every ounce of energy I could to help them move it, and finally it gave way beneath our combined efforts. As the door sprang open, the children poured out of the bus and swam to shore safely before they turned around to see the bus sink completely into the river. The next day, I saw an account of just such an accident in the paper and read with huge relief that all the children had gotten out safely. This was the first time that my astral experience had been confirmed by a media report. The thought that I had made a difference in the physical world—the sheer validation of it—was overwhelming. No matter how many times I see an account of something that has happened while I was there in ethereal form, it still amazes me.

When I'm working on the Night Shift, my conscious mind—the part of me that is most operative in waking reality—stays with me as a sort of passenger or observer. The conscious mind is curious. It likes to know how things work. But it also needs to be shown information in a way that makes it comprehensible to the graphic and literal waking consciousness. For the benefit of that mind, spirit teachers and guides will often give information in the form of a diagram superimposed over the body that shows the flow of energy and highlights the points that need energy relayed to them. Or they might offer practical information about herbs and diet by showing me an image of certain plants or foods, or giving me verbal directions. Sometimes images and words are combined to help me understand my advisors' directions. When I wake up, I can use that information as a basis for research. In this way, intuitive knowledge can direct and augment acquired knowledge. In the waking world, I pursue personal studies on healing and health. I must admit that a medical degree would be a great marriage with the energy work that I do. However, I do not have the diploma on my wall, and I want to emphasize again that I am **not** a medical doctor. Yet I still do as I have always done—I offer what help I can.

In order to sense and assess a person's emotional state, I place my hands on him, searching for the cold spots that indicate an energy blockage. Sometimes a word or an image of something inside the body accompanies this sensation. The moment I find the cold spot, the knowledge of what action to take comes to me in an intuitive flash. I may have the inclination to let my hands hover above the area or to lay them directly on the spot, sending a healing light, love, heat, color, or sound to that area. I may even be motivated to cover an area with stones and crystals in certain arrangements because of an image or phrase that one of my guides offers me. Each of these tools resonates at a unique frequency; I know which of them, or which combination of them, will be the most effective. Just as each situation is different, so each solution is tailored to the needs of the moment and the person.

For much of my life, I wondered if I worked alone on the Night Shift. In the way of the universe that ever seeks to bring us closer to the truth, one day I was sent an answer. I was completely exhausted, and was helping a boy while on the Night Shift when I felt a kind hand on my shoulder. The voice of a young man behind me said, "Here, let me help. You need to rest. You're not the only one doing this." He picked up where I left off, letting me take a much-needed break. Was he someone like me, on the Earth plane and dreaming, or was he a disincarnate soul? I still don't know, but I thank God for him. It doesn't matter to me if he is incarnate or not. It was simply good to learn that I wasn't alone.

Since then, I've seen many other energy healers on the astral plane. I've come to recognize them by the specific state of being—energy or vibration—that they emanate. We often give each other a look of acknowledgment as we attend to the needs of the moment.

Another benefit of working with fellow energy healers is that I've been able to experience what it's like to be on the receiving end of a healing. I was working with Carolyn, a mentor to whom my spirit guides "had" led me at a time when my doubts and conflicts needed to be resolved once and for all. My relationship with Carolyn and the benefits it brought to me are recounted in "Grey Wolf"—the chapter on guides—so I won't repeat it here except to say that, exhausted by the amount of energy it took to work the Night Shift, I was considering handing in my notice and quitting. Yet I knew that the repression of the vital, intuitive part of my being was not a solution and that, if I were to continue, I needed someone in the material world to help me learn how to reconcile aspects of my life that had been cohabitating less than comfortably. I had to find a way to balance my two roles: normal wife and mother by day and astral caped crusader by night. The mentor was with me when I realized that there was no quitting the Night Shift. For better or worse, the gift I had was a lifetime appointment.

I was sorely in need of some healing for myself, which my earthly mentor provided. With her direction, I opened up my consciousness to the subtle changes in my body and became aware that light bodies were coming together around me. Sometimes I felt an unseen presence, but at other times I actually saw a faint light body or a number of light beings laying their hands over or near me—sometimes right on and directly inside me. What I thought I knew of love on this earthly plane paled in comparison to what I felt during these healings. The unconditional love I felt was tangible and overwhelming.

Eventually I noticed that the light beings performing my healing were part of a team. Once the possibility of group effort was open to me, I warmed to the concept of calling upon other Night Shift workers for assistance in my own healing practice. Don't ask me why, but it had never occurred to me to ask before. It was a huge relief to know that there were others out there that could help me if I needed it. Making a request for assistance is a habit I now practice nightly as I prepare to enter the Night Shift. The spirits offer their help with infinite patience and generosity. The practice of group healing has reconfirmed the message that weaves in and out of the experiences and dreams I share with you: We are not alone.

My job is not easy. That is not a complaint, merely an observation. In my capacity as healer and rescue worker, I see so much suffering, so much pain. At times, it breaks my heart. I cannot save the world alone, much as I would like to. We heal what we can by recognizing our essential oneness and working together.

The circle of healing grows. Every act of compassion, yours and mine, small or large, adds to the glowing vortex that rises up to melt the world's ills in an ocean of light. That is the eternal promise of love.

CHAPTER 6

GREY WOLF

journaL entry
Saturday, December 27, 2003
As I l lie down and ready my mind to enter the Night Shift, I ask for an image that I can identify as a spirit guide.

The dreamtime opens, showing me Earth's moon, full and shining. Its gentle brilliance draws me into a peaceful and thoughtless contemplation, and so I gaze at it without expectation, just waiting.

The image of the moon begins to shift as I watch. Feathers form over its round and placid face, transforming it into the visage of an owl. The feathers are as softly colored as moonlight— gentle earthy umbers, buttery ochres and misty greys tinged with blue. Layer upon circular layer appear until the luminous orb is completely masked by them.

I sense a presence forming behind the mask. His essence is Native. He is completely hidden except for his eyes, which glow with wisdom, kindness, and understanding. They are the amber eyes of a wolf.

A spirit guide has come to my calling. His name is Grey Wolf.

Moon, owl, wolf. This nocturnal trio is richly layered with ancient meaning. The full moon is the vessel of divination and the womb of intuition—she lights the night sky, bringing the unconscious to consciousness, illuminating the darkness. She circles the Earth, marking for us the rhythms that gave rise to the earliest calendars. She pulls at the tides—not only of the seas, but also of our emotions. The reflective, knowing power of woman shines from her like a heavenly beacon as she watches over dreams and the mysteries of creative imagination.

The owl is a symbol for astral flight, magic, clairvoyance, and wisdom. Owl's vision can pierce through deception and uncover hidden truths. He brings messages in dreams or in moments of private meditation.

Deeply loyal, the wolf is sociable and generous, but also independent. He is strongly connected to the moon and all the power she holds. When he sings to her in the night, he calls down the inner power of the natural, untamed self that is an instinctive part of every human's earthly existence. Wolf is a great communicator and teacher.

I saw Grey Wolf only once. He didn't have a particular message for me, but I know guides only come to me for a specific reason. I'm not entirely sure why he made his appearance for this particular occasion, except to let me know that he is out there watching over me. His image has lingered in my mind ever since. Perhaps he looked over my shoulder as I painted his portrait. I would like to think so. In fact, it would have made the job a lot easier if I could have booked him for a sitting. Hopefully I got his features right. If I didn't, he hasn't complained.

My guides have been with me since childhood, sometimes as visible entities, sometimes as voices. Some of them come by often; others make an appearance only once, to help me with a specific problem or question.

Guides are pretty handy. I mean, who couldn't use a little advice now and then? What I really wanted before I had the Grey Wolf dream was to develop a system of communication with my guides—some way to get in touch with them when I needed help or had a burning question. I still don't have a formula for calling them up and requesting an audience whenever I want one. Rather, I've had to adopt what I call the "art of allowing" into my life, knowing my guides will drop me a line whenever *they* think there's something I need to know. They often show up at crucial moments to point me in the right direction, but more often than not they seem to think it's better to let me figure things out for myself.

There's a fine line between guides and teachers. Guides are entities that help you along on your personal journey. They're assigned to you based on your unique qualities and the purpose(s) for your present incarnation. Guides can appear as animals, people, or ethereal beings of light. They come to you in guises and forms that resonate with your particular essence and your chosen cultural experience.

Many people think that guides ease the pressures of decision that we all must make in our lives—but they don't. Guides don't tell me what will happen in the future. As nice as it would be for them to tell me what lottery numbers to pick, that's not the way it works. They can't be used for personal material gain, and they certainly don't command any sort of obedience. They won't make decisions for me—I have to do that myself, just like anyone else. They come to help, not to interfere with the free will that is so crucial a part of our journey on Earth.

I have a number of guides. It took me a while to figure out that they each have their specialty, and will answer questions relevant to their area of expertise. Some guides direct me in energy healing, while others show the way to a person I should meet. Some bring me information about herbs or diet or the use of crystals. Others come by when I need a moment of comfort or a companion for a brief leg of my journey.

I seem to have attracted a number of Native American guides. I wasn't always sure why that was until recently, when I was told by other mediums that I've spent an alternate life or two as a Native shaman and healer and that I am meant to resume my healer status in this time also. My Native American guides bring me to a better understanding of the gifts of nature, like herbs and healing crystals, and a closer relationship with Mother Earth and Father Sky. They also brought me an especially valuable gift in the form of a spirit name. I had been thinking about names— how they're so attached to identity, how women often take a new last name when they marry. Taking another's name gives you the strangest sensation that you are not quite yourself anymore—as if you have committed not only to a new relationship, but also to being a different person.

By the time I asked about my spirit name, my marriage was over. In my struggle to rediscover myself, I had returned to the artwork that had always formed a large part of my identity. Painters often consider how to sign their work, and I was thinking of using my maiden name— Monica Holy. Holy is a Czech name meaning "bare," as in a tree bare of its leaves. I thought the name quite apt for the new life I was forging—open to the elements, exposed, and waiting for the new growth of springtime. Of course, Holy has an English meaning as well, and this spoke to my deep connection to the spiritual life that stirred inside me, waiting to come to fruition when the season was right.

All the thoughts that whirled around in my mind about identity, art, spirit, and naming led me quite naturally to ask my guides, "Is there a spirit name you know me by?" I heard in reply a chorus of many voices. I imagined them waiting in the sidelines for just such a question so they could sing it out as one: "Moonaqua!" It sounded like a Native name. Since I don't have Native connections in this lifetime, I'm not sure why the name came at this time, but whatever the reason, I welcome it and keep it close in my heart. Getting a new name is a part of a rite of passage in many traditions—a sign of membership in a spiritual community.

Guides do so much more than offer spirit names— they can also offer life-changing suggestions. I'm truly grateful for the guide that asked me to make a simple phone call one day in 2003. Here's the story:

I was worried. I had fallen into a state of depression before, and I could feel the cycle about to begin again. I definitely didn't want to go there—my children needed me, and I needed to know I could be there for them. I had to heal whatever it was that had sent me into the downward spiral that was threatening to overtake me again.

I called out to my guides. "What can I do?" I asked. "Where can I find the help that I need?"

That was all I had to say. As soon as I finished my plea, a voice told me to call Carolyn Long, the life-changing mentor I've mentioned earlier in this book.

I had nothing to lose. I'd met Carolyn at a two-week business course I took in 2001. The course had been held in a beautiful old courthouse that had been converted into a community center. On the first day, the students entered the courtroom that now served as a theater and lecture hall, found their seats, and settled in as the lecture began.

It was an unexpected beginning. The instructor told us that some folks in the area thought the building was haunted. Apparently a court case in the 1800s had gone badly awry. A man named Jack was attending the trial of his son—or nephew, no one is quite sure which—who was on trial for rape. As the court awaited the verdict, Jack grew increasingly agitated. Unable to bear the pressure, he ran from the courtroom to the balcony outside. Just as the word "Guilty!" rang out through the hall, Jack tripped and fell over the balcony to his death.

Since then, there had been many reports of ghostly sightings around the building. Some said the ghost appeared in the shape of a black dog. Others claim to have seen an old man who walked with a cane. The instructor was obviously having fun with the story, telling us that there had been times in the past when people had run out of the room screaming. Smiling, he told us that if we *did* see something, we should remain calm. Naturally, I took the story with a grain of salt.

Later on, during a break, I made my way to the bathroom with a group of women. As we approached the door, a woman passed us, shivering slightly and remarking about how cold and freaky it was in there. One of us spoke up—a petite, almost tiny woman in her early fifties. She was smartly dressed, and her curly chestnut hair was cut to shoulder length. Her lively, intelligent brown eyes regarded the woman through rimless glasses.

"If there's a 'presence' you've encountered," she said, "you simply have to ask it if it's from the light. If it responds with a name, tell it with love that its time here has passed and that it needs to go to the light." She had more to say, but I was caught up by my own surprise. I had never heard anyone talk like that without coming across as a nutbar. She was completely unembarrassed by what was coming out of her mouth, but at the same time not in the least insistent. She simply offered advice on a strange situation as if it were the most natural thing in the world. "Wow," I thought. "This isn't your average bear." So I took note.

Over the next couple of weeks, both Carolyn and I were busy with the course material and lectures, but we observed each other, as students do. Carolyn stood out from the others. There was such an air of loving calmness about her that she struck me as someone who had been around the block, knew what she wanted and deserved, and had come into her own wisdom and grace.

I asked for her card, but it only listed her alternative healing practices like reiki, reflexology and therapeutic touch. Little did I know she was also a psychotherapist, certified hypnotherapist, past life regression therapist, and shaman. She spent many lifetimes as a Native shaman and remembers them well.

Now, months after the workshop, the voice of one of my spirit guides had advised me to get in touch with Carolyn. I called her, made an appointment, and wondered what on Earth I could say to her to explain why I wanted to see her.

We met at the local coffee shop. I hadn't prepared a speech. I hoped that when the moment came I would know what to say. I sat across from her in awkward silence for a few moments, but nothing except the raw truth came to mind. "Okay," I finally blurted out, "I don't know any other way to say this. I see dead people. I have no money. My guides sent me. Can you help me?"

She didn't even blink. "Why of course I can, dear," she said. "That's why I'm here." I felt like weeping with relief. I had finally told someone about my abilities, and the response I got was neither horror nor disbelief. I had a new guide—a flesh and blood one—to help me navigate the strange waters of my life. For the first time since high school, I had found someone I could confide in.

And so it began. After Carolyn had diagnosed me as not mentally ill, but as a medium and a healer, she told me that she would be giving me homework every week. She made it clear that she wasn't there to carry me; I would have to do my part, and if I didn't she would cut me loose. No nonsense and no laziness. She wasn't there to heal me;

I would be healing myself. Right from the beginning, she initiated lessons of self-empowerment, responsibility, and free will.

The next year was a marathon of learning—cranial-sacral work, reiki, acupressure, journey work, channeling, energy work, past life regressions. Carolyn was a fine and patient teacher. Observant and always present in the moment, she gives her students her full attention. She knows how to listen and when to speak. Soft-spoken yet firmly self-assured, her unconditional love comes across without the least hint of condescension.

I came to call her "Yoda" because she reminded me of the tiny wizened sage of *Star Wars*. "Don't think," she would say. "Just do!" Over the next year and a half, we assembled and filled a toolbox of exercises and practices as I learned how to direct my energies, balance my waking and dreaming lives, and understand the mechanics of my consciousness.

Carolyn also introduced me to another medical doctor and counselor who again determined that I was mentally sound. He referred to me as a natural-born shaman—a treetop shaman—because I had had no apprenticeship or teacher. I had learned by my own experiences. Although I was glad that there were names for what I did, I was also glad that I had not known them earlier. In a way, being in the dark about the details of my abilities had helped me to develop an attitude of non-expectation—just letting things come—that is key to the art of allowing.

It was during my work with Carolyn that I signed up for the Night Shift. I like to think that if there was a posting for the job it would have been something like this:

Wanted:
Emotional intuitive, empath, and lucid dreamer to work the borderlands. Must be committed to healing and guidance, able to deal with the traumatized dead.

Qualifications:
Apprenticeship from birth and before. At least thirty years experience in spirit communications. Dark night of the soul passed. Certification in grounding, electromagnetics, energy manipulation, benevolent intent. Experience in jump-in, push-thought, and border patrol preferred.

Apply within.

I remember the first day on the job in the dreamtime—the reading of contracts and the signing of papers and the confusion and stress common to any new job. I was going to work with guides and take classes and teach and answer the calls of souls in need. Although I had been active in the dreamtime since childhood, it had, until then, seemed like something that "happened" to me without my consent or understanding, like the requirement to go through elementary and high school. Now I was ready to embrace my path as a conscious and chosen decision—an entry into a cosmic university of healers and guides and teachers.

Signing up was a big step for me, a positive decision to work with the entities and energies entrusted to me. I entered a new commitment—a new relationship—with both body and soul. I don't consciously remember all the details of my contract (*way* too much fine print), but I do remember dreams that gave me clues.

It appears that, just as in the material world, the astral world has some sorting out to do when it comes to who will guide whom. I'm not sure who arranges it all, but the paperwork of my education and healing apparently got into a bit of an administrative tangle in those first days and nights. Somehow it's oddly reassuring that they can mess up on the other side, too.

Soon after I met Carolyn and accepted her as my earthly guide, I met a woman in the dreamtime who thought *she* was to be my guide. I was sitting outside a library—my dream symbol for "learning"—in something of a blue funk. The building behind me held such vast storehouses of knowledge and such a huge amount of ancient wisdom, that I was overwhelmed by how much there was to learn, how much to do. Was I capable? Could I really do this? I felt quiet, reserved, in a "bubble" frame of mind—curled into myself and brooding over what seemed like the monumental tasks ahead. A tall, slender European woman approached me, smiled, and said that she could see what was going on inside my head. She proved it by getting specific. She sent me a telepathic stream of information that was images of my own thoughts, my own feelings, my own memories. OK, I thought. She knows me, and I'm here to learn. What next?

"Come with me," the woman said, and turned to walk away. Thinking of Carolyn and my commitment to her, I wasn't very enthusiastic, but I followed anyway.

We mounted an open cart and floated through the city streets, coming to a halt at a run-down building, its surroundings strewn with broken glass, shards of brick, and cut wire. As the woman started inside, I stopped dead. I was barefoot, and feared that I would injure my body. Like I said, it was early in my career. I had a lot to learn about the fears and hesitations the waking mind can carry with it into the dreamtime reality.

The woman came back, a concerned look on her face. "I want to work with you," she said. "Your name has come up on the list."

"What do you mean?" I asked, but she only repeated that she wanted to be my guide through this—my journey through the early stages of my career in the Night Shift.

"You'll be working exclusively with me," she kept saying. "We'll be working together from now on."

I thought of Carolyn. Surely the question of guidance was already settled. I had been directed to the teacher I needed. The arrangement this woman was suggesting wouldn't be possible. I told her so.

"Who?" she wanted to know. "Who is working with you?" When I told her about Carolyn, the annoyed expression on her face said, "I should have been told about this."

"Your name was on the visitor list," she said. "You came up as visitor! Why didn't your name come up as taken?"

I didn't have an answer to her question, but she could see I wasn't going to budge in my decision and so, abruptly disappeared in what felt like the astral equivalent of a huff.

The arrangements and agreements that I made in the dreamtime were smoothed out over the next few years as I became acquainted with my many guides: **Shadow Hawk,** who gave me the chant "Canon Yoteh," which he later took as his name; beautiful, black-haired, willowy **Raven Claw,** a Cree woman who appeared to me dressed in cobalt blue beside a lake dotted with canoes; the unnamed young Native herbalist who brought me sweet grass and fresh lavender in a woven basket and taught me the ceremony of smudging; goat-footed **Pan,** wise with age, ancient god of shepherds and flocks, of mountain wilds, and of hunting and rustic music; golden-haired **Moonchild,** clothed in blue satin that flowed like water suspended in the air; **Desert Dude,** the brief companion who came to walk with me one night when I was uncertain of my path; **New Guy,** the blue-eyed black man who brought me rest and repose in a moment of exhaustion; **Wise Woman,** who told me, "Soon you'll be stepping on slushy onions," a humorous and cryptic message that told me that I would soon be losing the defenses that kept me from vulnerable and innocent understanding; **Doc,** skilled in matters of diet and bodily health; **Grandmother Moon** of the long white hair, who held a rattle in each hand and showed me objects of ceremony; the ethereal woman who helped me understand that faith in the moment is all I need to navigate the currents of life on both this side and the other; and **Moon-Qi,** master of crystals and energy alchemy and teacher of the power of mineral life.

Moon-Qi is one of my more frequent guides—one of the few who visits me in waking life. Although he generally stands behind me and advises in a whisper, I have seen him. He stands about seven feet tall and has blue skin. He wears a whitish, cowled robe. He's definitely *not* from around here.

I was introduced to Moon-Qi one summer afternoon in 2004 as I was trying to write in my dream journal. I couldn't seem to write a thing, and I was growing frustrated. I felt blocked, pent up with something I wanted to express and no words to do it with. Then I heard a voice.

"Go to the window for crystals and choose four of them," it said.

"Why?" I asked.

"Just do it," was the reply.

Who was I to argue? I went to the window and looked at the array of crystals and stones that were displayed there. "Which ones?" I asked. "Just choose the first four that come to mind," said the voice.

When I had made my choices—aventurine, blue, dragontooth, and moonstone—the voice said, "Put one on each corner of the desk." When I asked why yet again, the voice answered that it would create a flow of energy. It was not until then that I asked his name. "Moon-Qi," he told me. He was right about the energy flow: the writing block was lifted as I recounted my meeting with him.

Five nights later, I saw Moon-Qi again for a lesson in "energy alchemy." He showed me the three points on the side of the human head that are important in energy healing, and taught me how to stimulate these points.

One of my most unusual encounters with a guide came in January of 2007. The reason it was so unusual was that the presence that came to me wasn't even my own guide, but someone else's. The spirit wasn't exactly misguided—he was just being creative in getting a message to his charge.

Nikki had been trying to get in touch with her personal guide. She could sense when he was around, but was beginning to feel that the conversation was pretty one-sided. She told him that if he had something to say, he had to find a way to communicate with her. "Get creative, for cripes' sake!" was how she put it. Well, he did just that—by showing up in my dream in the standard black top and black pants worn by most of my guides. His outfit told me that he was a guide, but I was confused—I could sense that he wasn't one of mine. He told me that he was Nikki's teacher, and gave me this message: "Tell Nikki this: You're exactly where you need to be. You're on course. All the things you have done have put things in place where they need to be. All the things you've put in place fit perfectly with where Monica and all her things are. All the things you've had and now have in place have helped and have enabled all of Monica's things to be on course. The real estate, loft, and network of people are all there for a reason. It's all in place for you to do what you need to do and what you're already doing."

I gave Nikki the message the next day with a small addition. "Nikki," I teased, "you really missed out! This guide was gorgeous, just like your description of your dream guy—Egyptian and totally hot!"

Guides need to be resourceful as they try to communicate with us. If the direct route doesn't work, they don't just give up and abandon us. They try to find another way; or in some cases, a translator.

Everyone has guidance from Source. It's all around us—if we choose to notice it. This guidance doesn't always reveal itself through magical beings in glowing robes, and it's not always conveyed in English. Messages don't all hail from the dreamtime or the other side. Sometimes guidance comes into our lives via friends or even casual acquaintances who say something that answers a question we've been pondering. When that happens, I keep quiet and just take the message that has come to me through them. Guidance and synchronicities show themselves in everyday life and then wait patiently for us to take notice of them.

It's funny how we lend more credence to our "mystical" guides on the other side, as though their messages somehow carry more weight than messages we get from our fellow passengers en route to eternity right here on Earth.

Guidance comes in surprising and subtle ways—or sometimes not-so-subtle. Catastrophes, for example, can tell us to change our direction. If that is not guidance, what is? Our own unhappiness can be a welcome guide for the same reason. It tells us that something needs to change, that some new direction must be taken. Guides point. They point to the light. Again, they don't solve our problems for us.

In a sense, we can consider our entire environment a guide. Our presence in this existence—who we meet, what we do—*means* something. As we navigate through material existence, we ask, "But where am I going? Why am I going there?" Guides respond to questions like these. They may answer in a dream that you don't even remember, but which you wake up from with a lighter heart than you had yesterday. They may answer in a chance meeting that you have when you go out to get lettuce. They may answer in a newspaper article or the dialogue in a movie or the lyrics of a song on the radio. You never know where that message is going to come from, but if you're paying attention, you will notice it.

People wonder how they can get in touch with their personal spirit guides. As we move through life, we are surrounded by so many voices that demand our listening—voices of family, friends, schoolteachers, books, movies, media, newspapers, religion, science. We're assailed with voices from every side. To whom do we listen? How can we decide? How can we find our true guides?

Listening is crucial. So is looking. Guides thrive on awareness. If you are blessed with a modest guide, you may have to develop your listening into a fine and subtle skill. Practicing meditation really helps. As we silence the internal chatter that runs through our minds, we can then turn inward to hear our own truths and the voices of the guides that help us find them.

In my work on the Night Shift, I act as a guide as well as someone who's guided. I'm often drawn to young people at a crossroads in their lives, who need a push in the right direction. They might be contemplating trying drugs or joining a gang. I enter their minds and give a good hard push thought down the road that leads them to consider better choices.

I'm also aware of people close to physical harm. I've lost track of the number of times that I've guided someone who is in danger to a safe place that they hadn't seen in their panic—a closet or a side street that they would have passed by without a push thought.

Many people think of guides as entities from the other side. Clearly, however, many guides may be energy workers on the Night Shift who occupy the physical plane by day. As members of a collective consciousness, we help each other all the time. We are *all* Source energy, after all.

The guides that accompany us through life have their allies in the teachers that we encounter when we need them. You know the expression: When the student is ready, the teacher appears. Like guides, teachers are with us both on this side and in the dreamtime. They come into our lives much in the same way that guides do. Sometimes they just drop by to offer a brief lesson; at other times, we go to school intent on learning specific things.

When I signed up for the Night Shift, I agreed to take a number of classes. Astral education is not so different from earthly education. Fringe dwellers—one of the titles I go by in the dreamtime—go to classrooms and sit in front of blackboards and learn from experts. In the first days, students occasionally lose their way in the academic halls, just as I did when I stumbled into a room empty of students. The room had a haunted feel, and as I looked around I noticed that things were slowly disappearing from one spot, only to reappear in another. Once it had my attention, the movement began to increase in frequency and speed. Someone was trying to get through. The demand—the movement and the feel of the communication—grew in pitch. I felt an edge of aggression to it. Whoever was trying to come through was clearly frustrated, but I wasn't about to be intimidated! I dared the presence to show itself, even as it got more and more frantic. Our mutual frustration escalated until I got quite rude—shouting at it to come out and tell me what it wanted. I was practically shaking my fist. Suddenly a blank blackboard popped up next to a counter in the room. I went over to it, really angry by now, and slammed it down, shouting "That does me no good! Talk to me!" The blackboard loomed up again in front of me, still blank. There wasn't even any chalk to write with. Again I shouted, "What do you want?! This does me no good!"

The presence suddenly forced my hand down on a thin piece of pencil refill on the shelf in front of me. "What good will *this* do? It won't show up on a blackboard. It'll break!" I yelled out. "Write me what you want!"

The presence suddenly sent me stumbling backward with a good hard shove. The words "You write!" rang out from the middle of the room. For a few seconds, all was silent. Ooh...kay, I thought, I better just calm down. I let go, opening up to whatever the presence had to say. If nothing else, here was a little lesson in the art of allowing.

The presence proceeded to bombard me with an absolute overload of information. Hieroglyphs, symbols, images, and frenzied explanations started to overlap until I couldn't distinguish them in the massive confusion. In its eagerness, the presence advanced too close for comfort. I told it to slow down and step back because I couldn't focus on any one symbol long enough to decipher it. He didn't listen; he just kept coming closer and showing me more—filmy bubbles with symbols, squares, circles, and humanoid figures sliding over their surface. I tried to keep up as I madly jotted down what I could.

Much to my relief, the encounter finally ended. I didn't make much sense of the information the presence had shown me. All in all, it was a lesson gone very wrong. This teacher had proven too excitable to get his ideas across. I wondered if the classroom was "haunted" because other beings found this teacher equally difficult. I had learned one valuable lesson, though: to allow others to communicate in their own way and not to insist on how that might look. Ego had acted as a barrier between us.

My class the next night was very different. The room was full of students, the teacher relaxed and orderly. I felt young and green, like an adolescent. As the class began, the students paired up to choose the elements we wanted to work with on our first project.

The teacher wandered through the class, observing the students and reading his lecture out loud. I began to write notes, but noticed that I transposed some of the letters and words as I wrote. I wasn't sure if this was just a function of the different communication system I was using, or if there was something wrong with my comprehension. I figured the best way to find out was to ask.

When I raised my hand, the teacher seemed impatient at the interruption. Nonetheless, as soon as I said "When you were young, did you transpose?" his expression changed to one of sympathetic understanding. He came over to me and said, "Don't worry. You'll go through a lot of hard work and adjustment for the next year and a half, but then you'll be fine."

I settled in to listen and learn. By the time the class was over, the blackboard was filled with numbers, equations, formulae and writings. As the room emptied of students, I stayed behind to finish my notes. I felt older then, as if years had passed and I had learned a lot—more than just one class could have conveyed.

An Asian student came into the room. He studied the teacher's blackboard notes intently, and then stepped back and began to move in a dance-like, deliberate, repetitive manner reminiscent of tai-chi. He stopped periodically, looked at the board, and began again. I could see that his movements corresponded to the equations, and knew that I was watching something important—a physical interpretation of the abstract concepts on the blackboard.

I saw the teacher ambling down the hall, and quietly beckoned him to come back into the room and watch with me. He was mesmerized. As we watched, I explained my theory of what we were witnessing together: It seemed to me that the idea of chi—energy—was related to the material world not only through the mathematics on the board, but also through corresponding movements that reflected and activated that energy. The equations and movements related not only to the material bodies of individuals, but also to the world as a whole—to Earth and the energy forces that move through it. I got the sense that this energy pertains to all living things, to all of material existence, even down to the atoms and molecules that shape the universe as we know it.

I've been to many astral classes in which teachers have explained how energy works in abstract mathematical terms—from the medicinal properties of plants to the crystalline forms of minerals. Unfortunately, I don't usually retain the memory of these equations and formulae when I awake! I trust, nonetheless, that I've learned what I need to know for my job on the Night Shift. I use the information gleaned in astral school in the dimensions from which I receive it—the spaces on the other side of waking.

During the course of my ethereal education, I learned to apply and manipulate the magnetic forces used for propulsion in astral flight. I remember an early class in which I stood outside by a lake. As I looked out over the water, I felt myself "nudged" to float out over the surface of the lake. I did as I was prompted to do, but I was so overwhelmed by the new experience that I had problems focusing. I kept faltering, occasionally dipping into the water as I failed to maintain speed and height. More practice was clearly in order. My teachers were kind enough to turn the water into a sheet of ice—a solid form I could start with—like training wheels. In another class, I was told to paint a black runway and make a glass of water hover across it and around the room without spilling. The purpose of this and other classes was to gain the focus necessary for energy manipulation.

I've also attended a weekend camp to learn about crystals, divination, and pendulums, and taken classes in astronomy, the solar system and its planets, the universe, and the cosmos. But some of the most entertaining and fun classes have been the "energy ball" sessions. They're almost like playtime—students create balls of energy between their palms and bombard each other in a massive ethereal paintball game.

Students take tests in astral school, just as they do here. An especially memorable one took place in a park landscaped with expansive stretches of grass and bordered by trees. The lawns surrounded a huge rectangular lake. At one edge of the geometrical pool, a plain, box-like "building of knowledge" jutted out over the water's surface. Only its back was connected to the land. Water surrounded it on the other three sides, and the building had no windows. Neither were there doors, save for the large wooden ones at the front of the building, which I could see in the broad wall that rose from the middle of the lake. Four pillars flanked the doors, two on either side. The challenge was to enter a door. To make my way there, I would have to walk on water. The lessons kicked in, and I made my way across the water and through the doors to the book-lined halls inside the building.

I finally graduated—from those classes, at least. There are always more. Graduation from astral school entitles a former student to teach, and since then I've been instructing other energy workers in the arts of magnetism, energy, communication, and astral flight.

In one class, I was teaching students to focus their thoughts in order to change their state of being and their relationship to other elements. Again, water was part of the lesson. Students were learning to move on the water's surface by thinking of the top layer of water as an "accepting" layer of rubber-like resiliency. They understood from this lesson how elements can be manipulated by thought energy.

I had a dream that I was teaching in a beautiful large room. It was our first class meeting, and I was setting down the ground rules—a foundation of trust and honesty. I wanted my students to understand that we would all be learning from each other. Not only would they be learning from me—they would be teaching the class as well. My classroom was to be a forum of mutual exchange without a hierarchy of power between teacher and student. We were all equal.

I walked between the rows of students as I explained this. Each time I turned, I saw that the number of students had jumped exponentially. In the beginning there were about twenty. At the first turn, I saw that there were now forty. When I turned again I saw two hundred, and then two thousand. Whoa! Popular class. Who knew?

When the class ended, I was inside a cafeteria-style room with some of the students. We had done some energy work during class, and my feet were hurting something fierce. The students helped me take off my shoes, and as I removed one sock I could see scorch marks where the energy had coursed through the sole of my foot. Our roles were reversed—students were now teachers—as they showed me how to heal the burns. I was more than happy to get the astral equivalent of a foot massage! If you ever happen to scorch your feet with energy, I'll know what to do.

My beautiful and benevolent guides and teachers are a blessing. I'm graced to see and hear them—to know them in the way that I do—as beings that appear in human shapes that I recognize and understand. As glad as I am for all those that show up in human form, I know they're not the only ones guiding us. We have so much help, and it's all around us. To all the furred, feathered, and finned guides that creep, slither, leap, fly, or swim into our lives, I dedicate the next chapter, "Frog Medicine."

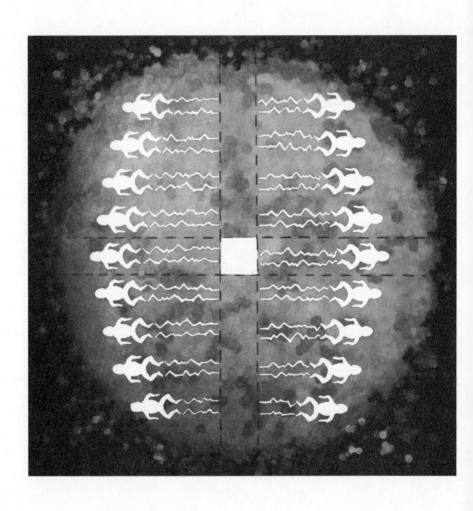

CHAPTER 7

FROG MEDICINE

journal entry
Friday, September 24, 2004

All I see before me is darkness. An image begins to take form, and I am infused with a stream of information. My mind can't keep up, but I know that my greater consciousness absorbs and understands it all.

The image begins as a square of green moss agate, the stone of healing and balance. Broken green lines emanate from each corner, forming a cross inside a circle. Frogs line the arms of the cross, squiggles coming outward from their feet. Frogs and squiggles vibrate at such an incredible speed that they glow a phosphorescent green, shimmering in the darkness.

I receive the overall simple message: "frog medicine."

The idea of frog medicine feels like something remembered, a retrieval of something long past.

From the beginning of our existence on Earth, humans have enjoyed a profound relationship with the natural world and the animals that inhabit it. We are ecologically and psychologically intertwined.

In many cultures, it goes without saying that we have much to learn from animals. More than that, shamanic tradition tells us we have power animals that bring us particular strengths and lessons that form a part of our essence. Our power animals are the ones that merge with us, become part of our being, and imbue us with their qualities.

People find their power animals during vision quests, in meditation, or in dreams. When we search for animal totems, we search for the part of ourselves that flows into the natural world without question or doubt—the part that just is. So when we find our animal totem, we find the part of ourselves that is complete, whole, essential, and inviolate.

The experience of allowing an animal to come into consciousness as an essential part of being human is profound. It changes our relationship with the animal kingdom, with the natural world, and with our natural selves. Power animals are instrumental in revealing our destiny and helping us along the path that is our true purpose in life.

We cannot choose our power animals; we must wait for them to come to us. The animals that appear may be surprising. I discovered this early in my sessions with Carolyn, when I was still getting used to the nature of the healing experience. Each session, though it followed a general outline, had a new perspective or a slightly different approach. I had come to Carolyn's office after a week's absence. In my week off, I'd experienced much that I felt needed work, so I'd been making mental and written notes throughout the week. Fully expecting to go through my list of concerns in a nice, orderly manner, I climbed onto Carolyn's massage table.

The session began as usual. We both grounded ourselves. Carolyn prepared herself for healing and I concentrated on slowing my breathing, relaxing, and calming the mind-chatter. When we were both ready, Carolyn asked me, "Where in your body do you feel discomfort?" She worked like that—no leading questions. She always asked me how I felt without putting ideas into my head. When something did come up—an image or a color or a sensation—only then would she gently nudge me down the path that the image or sensation suggested. From there, we would work it through.

This time was different. As soon as she asked the question, bam! Something entirely new came into my awareness, gaining momentum until it became the squeaky wheel that I couldn't ignore. Off we went, in a completely different direction than the one I'd anticipated.

I made a note to myself: "Stop preparing, anticipating, expecting, or assuming and *just allow*. Listen to your body. It will speak to you in the way it deems best. It will prioritize in a way that is beyond logic, so just strap yourself in, put your vehicle on autopilot, and let it show you where it, and you, need to go."

My lower and middle back spoke up loud and clear. Back pain was definitely not on my list of discussion points. Although I had been quite athletic growing up, chronic stiffness and constant pain had plagued me for many months. I dismissed it as the natural progression of age, or the result of long busy days. In other words, I did my best to ignore it. Now that was about to come to an end. Off I went, deeper and deeper into the feelings, images, colors, and sensations in that area of my body.

As I allowed the feelings to come through, I became hyperaware of the acute pain that I had tried so hard to ignore. I kept breathing, trying to work through it, but the pain didn't disappear—it grew. I saw dull and sullen colors painted on unyielding surfaces. The world receded into a tight ball of knotted flesh until it seemed that nothing existed except the pain. I wasn't sure that I could bear one more moment of it—and then an incredible thing happened.

I became aware that a giant lizard was hovering about a foot directly above me, its body parallel with mine. Suddenly, I forgot about the pain. I barely had enough time to think when—whhhhooooooooosh—the lizard dropped down into my body. I felt it merge its body with mine, moving through my chest to my back. In that moment it was not as if the lizard had become me, but that I had become the lizard. I could feel my body adapting to its curvy, elastic shape; my spine became sinuous and lithe. I felt as if I had absorbed the very essence, spirit, and nature of the lizard—that I had become one with it.

Since then, the feeling of "lizard" has always been with me. It's like I've acquired a new part of myself. My deep-rooted respect for this creature—what it stands for, what it brought to me—has stayed with me. In my mind, that means that I possess flexibility of both body and spirit.

When the experience was over and Carolyn brought me back to the waking world, I was astounded by how different I felt. For the first time in years, I felt no pain. I actually understood what it was to be limber, to enjoy freedom of movement. As with a lot of sessions, time had taken on new proportions. What felt like five minutes had lasted for over an hour. I had journeyed through a rigid, stiff block and come out the other side liberated from an oppressive weight.

It is said that if a lizard appears in meditation or is revealed as your totem animal, you should trust your intuition and pay attention to your dreams. Once the power of the lizard had descended into me, the self-distrust I had harbored in my body as back pain disappeared. The stiffness of trying to bind myself to others' rules, rather than trusting my inner knowing, simply melted away.

A few months after the lizard experience, Carolyn and I were working on my standing in my own power. The goal was to get to a place where I wouldn't need anyone's approval, love, or gratitude—that would all come from me. I was learning to accept other people's behaviors as theirs, not mine—learning to not take others' actions and words personally.

I was on the massage table, grounding and centering myself. As I went deeper and deeper into the meditative state, a wondrous creature revealed itself to me.

I saw a huge dragon whose skin of rich, deep red had the worn quality of old leather. I could tell how powerful she was, but I wasn't afraid of her one bit. I felt only awe and respect. She wasn't threatening; she crouched in a lazy comfortable repose, just *being*. Her skin was so thick that it seemed no weapon could penetrate her hide, yet she also had the vulnerability of her belly, where the skin was softer, more tender, penetrable. Even though it was clear that she was fully capable of unleashing a stream of fire from her breath, I knew she wouldn't unless she needed to. Just as people who master martial arts know the purpose of the practice isn't to show off or become the bully, the truly empowered know that if they need to call on defensive skills, they can.

Carolyn saw the dragon's presence as an opportunity for learning. She took me through the process of becoming the dragon, and taught me to understand the true meaning of the concept that standing in your own power doesn't mean you need an aggressive, in-your-face attitude. It means allowing the essence of your true self to come through. "Once you understand yourself at a very deep level, everyone else will understand you, and you won't have to say a word!" she said. That is one of the lessons of the dragon.

Carolyn also told me to become the dragon when I heard my inner critic begin to nag at me. By asking my subconscious mind to blend and harmonize my inner support system, I would be able to gently but firmly still the voice of my inner critic. Once you have the experience of taking in the essence and energy of a totem, it's with you forever. It's part of you and will lend you its wisdom.

Animal guides do not meld with you in the same way that power animals do. They help and protect you on your journey through life. We can sometimes recognize animal guides when an especially strange or noteworthy incident involving an animal takes place in daily life—something that makes us sit up and take notice.

I was once on a 22-mile hike with my father through Algonquin Park—a huge, 2,946 square mile expanse of forests, lakes, rivers and, of course, wildlife. We were walking along the trail when a moose popped its head up from the brush. Now, moose are large animals—very large. You don't want to mess with them. So there was what I thought was a pretty big moose in my path, when from just behind it, mama moose popped her head out of the trees. This wasn't looking too good! Then papa moose showed up. He had a rack of antlers on him wide enough to span a two-lane highway—or at least it seemed that way to me. My father and I stood there, wondering what to do. It wasn't something I was thinking about at the moment, but very slowly my dad handed me his camera. "Here," he said. "I don't have my glasses on. You take the picture." Well, I did, but that didn't solve the problem. The moose family was in no hurry to move, so I did the only thing that came to mind: I walked towards them, clapping my hands and asking them to move. They finally did, but by then it was getting late.

Algonquin Park is, as I said, huge. It turned out that the map we had with us was wrong, and we weren't where we should have been. We'd been dawdling when we should have been hustling on our 22-mile day hike, and my dad's knee was starting to hurt. It was getting late in the afternoon. We realized we had lost the trail, and we hadn't come prepared for an overnight stay (ironic for me, an ex-scout leader who should have known better). I was starting to get worried. Just then, a fox appeared 20 feet ahead, sat down, and looked at us. It seemed like he was trying to tell us something, so we decided to take the hint. We headed towards him. The fox took off, but just before he was out of sight, he sat down and looked at us again. We followed, and he kept running ahead and waiting for us until we reached the trail. Then he disappeared. What can I say? Thanks, Fox, for being a guide in such a literal way.

I haven't seen Fox again. He appeared to us for a specific occasion, as some animal guides do. Other animal guides come by again and again. They become familiar friends. I've met the frogs that showed up in my frog medicine dream a number of times. I interpret the dream as a picture of frog *energy* (symbolized as "squiggles"), an introduction, so to speak, to the powers of a guide that has shown up in my life many times since.

The frog's message has been, and continues to be, one of transformation.

What is transformation? It seems like a simple question with a simple answer: It is changing from one form to another. Throughout our lives, we constantly experience transformation. No hour is the same as the last; no one day is like another. When we discover the newness of each moment, the world of possibilities opens up to us.

Sometimes we forget to notice the newness of each moment or each day. The change is so slow that we forget it is happening. We become so caught up in the habit of our rituals—when we rise, when we sleep; what we eat, and when; how we choose our clothes and plan our day—that we see only the sameness, and not the change.

But sometimes transformation is dramatic. Maybe we lose someone precious—a friend or a spouse or a child or a parent—and we know that now everything is different. A transformation has taken place. Sometimes people say their eyes have been opened and we know that it means they've had a revelation—a sudden awakening or insight. Perhaps they have had an inspired idea or a dream—a gift of understanding that seems to fall from the sky. In an instant, their world is not what it was before.

Transformation of the soul is a reconfiguration of understanding. Change is inevitable, an aspect of incarnation. Everything that lives changes. It might be a slow, gradual change, or it might be as swift as the arrow that flies from the taut bow and meets its target. Either way, it happens.

The frog has been a symbol of transformation in most cultures because it changes its form during the course of its life—from water-dwelling tadpole to land-hopping frog. Frog is said, therefore, to exist in two worlds. Shamans tell us that the leap of a frog is like the leap from one spiritual realm to another. Frog energy is powerful. Frogs are highly sensitive to changes in the environment, so they tell us when things are out of balance, when the transformation of healing needs to take place.

It was a couple of years after my dreamtime introduction to frog medicine that the frog came into my life again. I became interested in a drumming journey workshop offered by Chris Poellien, a Reiki master, shaman, and world-class skier who has studied metaphysical concepts and meditation for over twenty years. Deeply rooted in totem animal experiences, Chris approaches the guided drumming journey as a vision quest or discovery, and I can't argue with that. I had visions and discoveries galore while on a retreat at her Sun Raven Wellness Center during the summer of 2005.

A group of women had gathered on Pender Island in British Columbia to take part in the weekend-long retreat. Chris began by outlining the three stages of the journey. In the first stage, we would be visiting the Lower World. Here, we might meet our totem animals, fairies of the land, or guardians of the earth. The next stage was the Middle World, realm of our guides and ancestors. The last stage was the Upper World (the star nation, or our higher selves), where we might encounter angels and ascended masters.

We began by visitng a sacred place, a Native burial ground located near Chris' wellness center. She told us to look for our personal entrance point to the Underworld. This could be a knot in a tree, a tangle of roots, a cleft in a rock, or a depression in the ground—any place that resonated with our idea of an Earth entrance. We would picture that doorway as we went on our journey.

We then returned to the center to begin. Since this was our first time, we were to set our intention to meet our guide and travel with it to wherever it led us. The guide, she explained, could be a creature of any sort.

Chris had us lie down comfortably on the floor, hands by our sides, eyes closed. She began to beat rhythmically on the drum as we slowed our breathing, focused, and relaxed.

My shamanic journey began as I saw my entrance point. I approached the cubby hole I had seen in a rock at the burial ground and—whhhhhoooooosh—down I went into a black hole. I was suspended in the pitch black. I felt like I was standing, but it was hard to tell. I couldn't distinguish walls from floor; it was all the same blackness. I patiently waited until I saw a figure appear not too far from me.

Picture a tall, thin, gangly frog that walks on his hind legs like a human—but in the most rubbery, elastic, and fluid manner. He is green, and wears a black tuxedo with tails. He has a huge grin spread across his face. I smiled, too—I was loving this! I had a funky new guide from the underworld all dressed up for the occasion. I didn't have a chance to converse, though. I heard the four drumbeats that signaled it was time to come back and prepare for the next stage.

We all wrote down what we had experienced and lay down again for the next stage—the Middle World, where we might meet spirits and guides who could help us in day-to-day life. I was waiting in blackness, again not knowing what to expect. Not too far in front of me, I saw a little tree frog leap in slow motion out of the blackness and land by my feet. I looked around and saw other color-ful tree frogs emerge out of the blackness from all sides. When they reached my feet, they started climbing up my legs—scores of them—until they covered my entire body. It felt incredible. They emanated an energy buzz that left a residual tingle on my body wherever they touched. I found myself turning in a horizontal position, magically suspended in the blackness as these wonderful creatures continued to clamor all over me. Then I felt a healing take place—a wonderful, cleansing, re-energizing feeling. I was just reveling in the sensation when I heard the drum calling us back.

We'd be going to the Upper World next. I had a question for any of the spirits I might meet there. I had been thinking of Middle Earth, the name Nikki and I had given to the artist's and writer's retreat we wanted to establish. My question was, "Where do we build our Middle Earth?" I waited patiently, allowing myself to drift with the rhythm of the drum as a scene unfolded before me.

Middle Earth revealed itself out of the blackness. I saw a beautiful cob structure standing in a glorious meadow where the sun shone brightly. I then found myself inside the house, the front and back doors both open. As I stood there, a lone frog jumped in through the front door and leapt in graceful slow motion from floor to kitchen counter to living room table, and then past me and out the back door. No sooner had he disappeared when another frog came in through the front door and repeated the slow motion journey to the back. Another quickly followed, and then another, until the croaking, chirping frogs were flooding through the entrance, leaping over and under each other in a raucous migration.

"Hey!" I interjected, thinking of Nikki's reaction to all these suction-toed creatures clamoring over her copper pots and cutlery. I guess the domestic diva in me kicked in. The response out of the shadows was clear. "Middle Earth will be a place of healing." I must confess I was dismayed by this suggestion of a change in my plans. "No!" I said, "Middle Earth is where my art studio will be. I'll be doing my art here." Again the voice said, "Middle Earth will be a place of healing." I argued for a while, but the answer I got was the same calm, unchanging reply. "Oh, for crying out loud," I said, "but I *still* want to have my studio here." There was no arguing. "Middle Earth will be a place of healing!" insisted the voice one last time. "Okay, *okay*. I get it!" I said at last. Sometimes there's no arguing with guides, no matter how much I want things my way.

The drumming journey was over, and it had been full of surprises. Not only had a charming gentleman frog introduced himself, but the guides had also given a new purpose to Middle Earth.

I've heard from Frog several times since then, and gotten to know him a little bit better. He's attracted by the drum. He shows up to drumming journeys like he's coming to a soirée, all dressed up in formal wear. On a more recent drumming journey, he'd added spats to his elegant outfit. I half expect a top hat next time, or perhaps a jaunty cape he can throw over his shoulder as he points the way with a silver-knobbed cane. He's very much the gentleman.

He especially enjoys communicating with me through synchronicity, I suspect because it is such a playful way of communicating.

Frog showed up again on a subsequent drumming meditation when I was told by a guide to "go to the Queen Charlottes to hear the frogs singing." I didn't rush off to the islands; I mean, it was a *heck* of a long way to go to hear singing frogs! But I did take note of the message. Here were frogs again, hopping into my awareness, and now the guides had added the name of a place to the mix.

A few weeks later, I went to an art gallery with a friend to see a Haida art exhibit. I was hoping for clues and answers to the whole frog connection. I met a well-known totem pole carver, who proceeded to tell me about the frogs on the Queen Charlottes. A boy, he said, had originally brought them over and their population had grown to huge proportions. He described the time he was driving through the islands decades ago and heard a deafening roar. He got out of his Jeep to see the entire surface of the ground shuddering with the movement of frogs. That was quite an image, and naturally it stuck in my mind. Since then, he said, the frogs had almost disappeared, but now they were making a comeback.

Not long after that, Nikki and I went to a screening of *The Secret* at a Spiritualist church with a friend. We had settled in quietly at one of the tables when a woman at another table leaned over and gingerly said, "I normally don't do this. I'm a medium. I don't practice professionally anymore, but my guides instructed me to tell you that you're supposed to go visit the Queen Charlottes. Masset, to be exact." Whoa. It seems there were a lot of guides involved in this, and not all of them were mine.

Our next hint came at the planetarium, where along with the exhibit there hung a huge poster for a contest to win a trip to the Queen Charlottes. Nikki and I didn't win, but the poster was another synchronistic tap on the shoulder. There was definitely no ignoring the message. The guides were going to keep strewing those bread-crumbs until we went.

We began to plan our trip. Nikki called a Native acquaintance from work and asked him if he knew anybody in the Queen Charlottes. Yes, he told her, and went on to say that he was Haida and that his family lived there. He had friends who were elders and lived on the reservation, where they ran a bed and breakfast. Would we like to stay with them? And oh, by the way, they're in Masset.

Whoever arranges these things was making it very easy for us. Off we finally went to the magnificent islands that sit in the Pacific Ocean just south of Alaska. Today the Natives call these islands "Haida Gwaii," or Land of the People. The more ancient name was "Xhaaydla Gwaayaay," meaning Islands on the Boundary between Worlds. What a perfect place for a fringe dweller such as myself to go.

The islands were lush and thick with the sense of ancient places. I was lulled to sleep by frog song. Sometimes primary guides step back and let others sing the aria, and so it happened on our stay on the Queen Charlottes. I had been invited there to listen to the frogs sing, and they did, but only as the peaceful lullaby of nature that lets you know as you fall asleep that you are in her arms.

Frog had led me there, but other, non-froggy guides showed up three times during our stay on the islands. The first time, Nikki and I were on a walk when I got a message to collect healing rocks with high energy for Middle Earth. The stones I was directed to gather were large and heavy, and I took some time to argue with my guide about the difficulty of carrying them the distance back to the car and then back to Vancouver. Guides have a way of forgetting the limitations of the material world, and this one was more excited about healing crystals than my back or legs. He kept insisting, but I finally out-stubborned him and got him to show me smaller stones that would suit the purpose.

The second guide visit happened while Nikki and I were at a hot springs. I heard a voice say that I was "there for a healing." I hadn't been aware that I needed a healing, but five days later, a boil appeared on my chest, as if an infection buried deep within my lungs had come to the surface where it could be released and healed.

The final guide appearance was at an ecological reserve on the island. As I was wandering down a quiet path of pine needle and leaf, I felt a beckoning to go into the forest that lay thick on either side. I sat on a log, intending to just be still in the moment. The sun filtered down in gentle beams through the canopy overhead, and the forest rustled with its subtle sounds of nature. Suddenly, my perception shifted and the trees that surrounded me started flickering in and out of transparency. It wasn't the frogs that sang then, but the spirit of the trees. I heard the voice say "tree spirits" and felt an incredible sense of the trees' living, conscious presence, green and rooted, smelling of loam and history. The voice of the trees was collective, aware, and as ancient, it felt, as Earth herself. Vegans will be very dismayed to know that everything has spirit in it.

For all his playfulness, Frog brings a powerful message of sensitivity to the environment, especially in regards to the symbolic water of emotion. Some say that Frog represents the cleansing power of tears, so if he comes into your life, you may find yourself susceptible to a new vulnerability. That's part of his message.

But Frog isn't everyone's guide. We all have specific lessons to learn from our power animals. There are as many types of guides as there are animal species. And that includes insects! There is no right or wrong guide to have; no one that is better than another. Every species on Earth has its own particular wisdom to bring to us.

Our totem animals are indicators not only of our personal power, but also of our direction in this life. My guides have told me that I have been a healer many, many times, and that my path is not so much about re-learning these skills (since I've had them since birth) as it is about remembering them—the same feeling I got when I dreamt of frog medicine.

The recurring symbol of frog medicine has taken over the direction of my life, leading me back to my path as healer. Every dream, drumming meditation, and spirit voice I hear, every synchronicity I witness, is leading me farther along toward my true destiny. No doubt Middle Earth will become a place of healing. What shape that healing will take is still uncertain, but I *am* certain that guides, including the animals, will continue to show me the way.

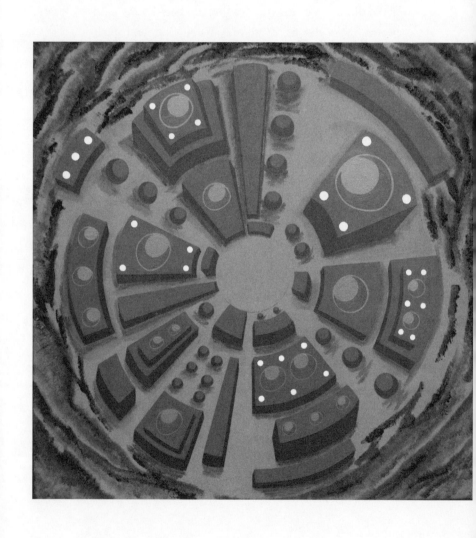

CHAPTER 8
MARS

јournaL entry
Wednesday, March 5, 2003

I feel myself drifting high above a planet. I let the current of the planet's orbit draw me closer to it in a sweeping arc until I am near enough to see what I can only describe as a wondrous city below me. I know that I am looking down on Mars.

The layout of the city is circular, streets curved and buildings shaped like wedges. Some of the buildings are topped with large domes and smaller silvery nodules. All the buildings emanate from the central space, which I sense was once a gathering place for whoever lived there—but there are no inhabitants visible, for this city has been empty of living creatures for years beyond counting.

I am filled with admiration for the simple functional geometry of the city. It looks as if it has been designed ergonomically: the patterns of streets and structures are meant to encourage the easy flow of movement. I get a sense that the inhabitants moved in a choreography of awareness of each other so serene that they strode without hesitation through these streets.

Nor does the city fight with its surroundings. It fits into the rust-colored landscape with ease and grace. There are no walls at the perimeter. Instead, the city sits in a crater that acts as a natural retaining wall. The land at the edge curves upward and flows out into the environment without barriers.

The expanses of land around the city are barren and empty. Everything is utterly still and silent. I am looking down at a ghost town, but there is no sense of abandonment or loss in that understanding. The feelings lodged in the architecture of the individual buildings and the city as a whole are of love, peace, knowledge, and understanding.

So much of my time on the Night Shift is taken up with the serious business of helping souls in distress and healing those still on Earth that it's a bit of a surprise when I find myself on a short pleasure cruise, a little magical mystery tour.

The image of Mars and the city on its surface stays with me. It looked so at one with its environment, so still in shape and feeling. There was nothing to tell me how long the city had been there, no clue as to when or why it had been abandoned. Still, I could feel the imprint of civilization embedded in the russet-colored walls below me, could sense the movements of those long-gone beings in the streets of the city they had built. It was odd, the simultaneous sense of stillness and movement that I found there.

The possibility of life on other planets is hotly debated by scientists, and Mars has always been in the forefront of this debate. From the mid-seventeenth century, when expanding and shrinking polar ice caps were first observed on the planet's surface, to the recent space probes that have found evidence of fossilized water-dependent organisms, speculation about Mars continues. Those who believe that there was an ancient race on the planet talk in terms of billions of years—timelines so vast that we have a hard time grasping them from the perspective of our young culture.

Do I believe in aliens? Do I believe that the city I saw on Mars was built by an alien race? I would say yes, except I don't really care for the word "aliens." I wouldn't call a bird an alien because its shape is not the same as mine. The worlds and spaces I move through include many life forms and many types of beings, but we all inhabit the same universe and we're all part of one continuing unfolding creation. We're all part of the fabric of being; nothing that exists is alien to that fabric. The citizens of Mars, or any other planet, are simply neighbors who live a little farther away than most.

Reaching across such great distances usually involves complicated preparations of machinery and years of effort by many scientists, but there are easier and quicker ways to get there. When we enter a dream, we take on the lighter density of an ethereal being. Unconstrained by the physical body, we can breathe underwater, enter a cell, or hover over the surface of a planet light years away from Earth. We can fly. In dream reality, space as we know it loses meaning, and we can move across the room or across the universe with the swiftness of a thought.

If you recall having a dream in which you are flying, the experience of moving through space on the wings of a thought may be more familiar to you than you think. There are plenty of ways to get around astrally—personal styles of flight devised by the individual spirit. Some people flap their arms and hop up and away like a bad Wright brothers experiment. Some breathe into their diaphragm and float up like a helium balloon. Heck, you could grow a propeller on your head and whirl your way around town if you wanted to. Flying in the dreamtime is whatever you want it to be; the only limitations are those of imagination.

Most of us have to learn the skills of flight from more experienced spirits, but some of us are naturals, such as my son Alexander. I realized this years ago. When he was a small boy, only four years old, I recall seeing him show up in the astral plane a number of times. One night as I was dreaming, I saw Alexander flitting about our house as it looked in the waking reality, going from room to room. I chased him until I caught up to him in the bathroom, where he was hovering above the window, inches from the ceiling. He was all grins and smiles, but the mom in me kicked in and I became concerned that he was too young to stay out of his material body for so long. "Go on back now," I told him firmly in my best mom voice. Like a typical child, he reluctantly took himself back to the small body sleeping upstairs. The next day our dream came up in discussion. "Did you see me, Mommy?" he asked. "Did you see me?" Of course I said I had because it was true, but I kept thinking, "Here we go again!" My child had apparently inherited my natural abilities to enter other-worldly realms. Time will tell where he goes with them.

Recently I asked Alexander, now a senior in high school, if he recalled having any out-of-body experiences as a child. He immediately began to talk with enthusiasm about all the times he remembered darting around the house while his body lay upstairs in bed. "I was definitely a ceiling cruiser," he said. He told me that he would drift off and follow me around the house as I looked after the domestic business of the day.

I then asked him if he remembered meeting me outside the house on his night flights, and indeed he did. He recalled some incidents that I had forgotten, and I remembered some that he had—like the night when I was deep in the borderland. I was immersed in blackness when I saw an island of green vegetation appear. My young son was on it, laughing and having fun. I was immediately worried. "Alexander!" I yelled. "Stay where you are! I'm coming to get you." I headed toward him, but he disappeared and reemerged on a new island somewhere else. For him, it was a great game of hide-and-seek. He giggled with delight as he kept disappearing and popping up in new places, while I grew more and more worried that he might get lost down some wormhole and not know how to find his way back. If there was ever an ethereal hand-wringing going on, that was it. Obviously, he made it back safely and I awoke amazed by the level of skill he had shown in navigating the invisible currents and layers of reality.

My own mastery of flight took a bit more effort. As an adult, I attended dreamtime classes to learn the finer points. In one class, I practiced maneuvering through air currents in a wind tunnel specially constructed for the purpose. In my ethereal form, the air felt as thick and buoyant as water, and I soon became adept at shifting my direction and speed. I also learned to use electromagnetically charged surfaces to hover, and later to move while hovering. Once I'd gotten the hang of a few forms of flight, I was able to teach others.

Flight education is not always smooth. At times it's like watching nestlings as they tumble from the nest on their first wobbly journey to a nearby branch. I recall being with a group of schoolmates who were testing their skills, first from a tree and then from the ledge of a house. One girl was bold enough to launch herself from the top of a building. I only had time to watch anxiously as I frantically sent her last-minute instructions, but her ambitions outstripped her skill. She plummeted! At the last possible moment, she managed to slow her descent and landed on the ground with a thud. She got up unharmed and walked away—a bit sheepish, but ready to try again.

In my capacity as a healer, teacher, guide, and ethereal tourist, I've adopted a number of ways to get where I need to go. I've spread the wings of a giant red pterodactyl whose form I borrowed, just to see through those ancient eyes and feel the wind on my leathery skin. At times I soar over the Earth with arms outstretched. I pass over the landscape as a bird does, skimming the treetops and occasionally swooping down for a closer look. Or I might actually sprout a pair of huge feathered wings, as I did when I took a young man for a ride. He was becoming a pretty serious bully to his classmates and needed to get a larger perspective on the world, so I took him on a short trip. As we flew through the night, he avidly watched the spirit interactions that took place in the wider reality, and I think he began to understand our essential unity. The longer he was immersed in an atmosphere where he could sense the love that holds up the universe, the more the brittle armor of his anger and sense of victimization melted away. He gave in to his wonder, and when he had seen enough, he fell asleep between the giant wings, as trusting as a cradled baby.

I include levitation as a type of ethereal travel, but it's not one that I've experienced with great frequency. My most vivid memory of it began one night as I felt my whole body start to vibrate in a way it never had before. My eyes were closed; my mind was in the borderland of a lucid dream. The vibrating increased until my entire body felt charged with electric energy. The intensity rose to such a pitch that I lifted off the bed, suspended above it. Gravity was replaced by a push/pull of polarities, so light and natural that the push and pull were unified even in their opposition. I felt a perfect balance of physicality immersed in space. I woke up later with the certainty that levitation could happen even in the physical, waking reality.

Levitation has been the subject of anecdotal evidence from numerous cultures throughout history and has been featured in sacred writings from around the globe. Opinions are divided—some attribute it to devilish forces, others to the powers of saints and mystics. Many believe that levitation is the trick of illusionists intent on trickery and the picking of pockets for their own gain. More recently, as scientists' understanding of the laws of gravity expand, some physicists are exploring the possibility of levitating objects. What they find could give new meaning to the phrase "castles in the sky."

In most forms of ethereal travel—from bird to levitation—I have a sense of my physical body, which retains its shape in ethereal form. However, there is another style of travel in which all sense of the corporeal body is lost. I call it Eyes and Mind. When I travel this way, I become only vision and consciousness, able to go incredible distances at tremendous speed. At the beginning of this flight, I'm on an astral highway and can see the landscape passing by. Even as the speed of flight increases, I can still make out the objects that are part of the scenery. I set my thoughts on a destination—a time and a place—that I want to reach. Suddenly, I become a white streak passing around and through objects at lightning speed. Everything becomes a blur and I hear a distinctive hum. Almost instantly, I'm there. I quickly slow down and come to a halt.

This kind of travel depends on my ability to let go of the idea of the human shape (not always easy) and become only a seeing consciousness. As Eyes and Mind, I can enter a person's body (with permission, of course!) using his or her eyes as a conduit. I'm able to travel inside the person's body to see physical structures on a microscopic level—cellular, molecular and genetic—to repair misalignments, if that's what's needed. Or I can jump in during an emergency to influence events. If a person is in danger, about to be accosted for instance, I may be able to warn them and point out a quick escape route. Jumping in is like merging with another person on several levels—physically, mentally, and emotionally. I resort to it only in extreme situations.

Eyes and Mind can be a lot of fun. I've played with it by zipping around a room like a ping pong ball, bouncing off walls and ceiling and floor. Once I even popped into a bottle and looked out at the room through the curved green glass, feeling like a genie.

My portal to other dimensions is the half-sleep that is lucid dreaming. Lucid dreaming is that state of consciousness where it is possible to be simultaneously aware of material and non-material realities, and to function in a conscious way from the energy, or astral, body. These dreams can be induced in just about anyone, and dreamers can develop methods to enter that particular state. I effortlessly and frequently fall into them and have always done so.

Lucid dreaming has been well studied by scientists. They have plenty to say about brain waves and REM sleep, but I hardly think about those things as I approach the brink of the borderland. Since I have jobs to do, I prepare myself for the busy night ahead by grounding myself, sending roots deep down into the earth and also out into infinite space. Then I thank my guides, and ask for protection from any dark energies that I may encounter. I ask any light beings wishing to help me to come forward, and then I still the mind-chatter that has filled my waking hours. I'm ready to enter the Night Shift.

I open the door between waking and sleeping. Dream images begin to appear. I have a heightened awareness of the small noises around me—a cat meowing outside, a car driving off in the distance. Those noises fade as I enter the Night Shift. I am in between worlds, allowing me to work with the energy that affects earthly life from the other side. The door that usually closes between waking and dreaming reality remains open. I am both here and there, aware of the interpenetrating realities of wakefulness and dreaming.

What feels like an electrical surge moves through my entire body, starting with my fingers and toes. The current moves through me at an incredible speed until it surges up my neck and releases itself at the base of my skull with a "snap" from left to right.

Instantly, my consciousness is surfing the frequencies of the spirit world, searching the airwaves as if on a radio for a specific channel. I'm reaching out for any sensation that signals that somebody needs my assistance, and when I feel it, I respond. If there are no calls out at the moment, my consciousness is free to explore places like the vast marbled halls of the eternal records of all humankind, or the abandoned city of Mars.

Space explorers haven't seen anything like the city I saw on the surface of that planet—yet. Perhaps that is because travel in the astral plane occurs outside the rules of space *and* time. Our idea of time as a railroad track along which we move in one direction from birth to death doesn't apply there. In that reality, past, present, and future all exist at once and it is possible to enter different time frames.

I picture time as a sphere that emanates out from our being. We humans are at its center, generating past and future from the eternal now. Strangely, in my picture the past is unfolding and "future" lives have already been lived. I'll talk more about simultaneous time and its relationship to healing in the final chapter, "The Grid." In the meantime, I just hope *someone* is keeping track of the frequent flyer points.

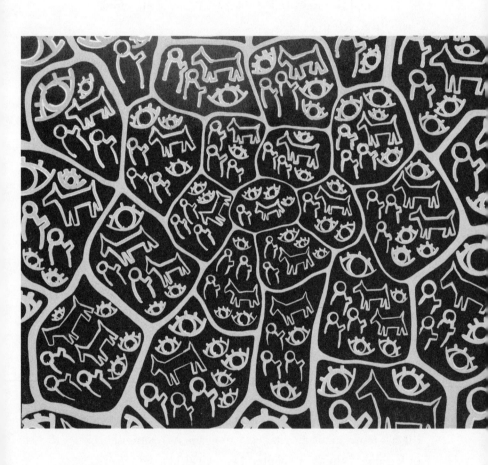

CHAPTER 9

SYNCHRONICITY

journal entry

Wednesday, November 20, 2002

Crack! I'm awakened from a deep sleep by what sounds like someone quickly and forcefully smacking their hand down on the armrest to the left of me. Adrenaline racing, I don't know what to expect.

Time passes.

Nothing happens.

I'm half-awake now, glancing around the room. Quite frankly, I'm not used to wakeful interaction while on the Night Shift. When I close my eyes, I'm hoping for either communication or a return to sleep. In complete contrast to my feelings earlier, an overwhelming sense of trust descends upon me. I feel totally safe.

My eyes are closed, but I can see through my eyelids as if they are open. Uncertain if this is just an image made up in my mind or if it's really happening, I open my eyes for a moment. Yup—it's out there. I close my eyes again and scan the room. An intense, phosphorescent glow begins to shape itself into a web of cells, each filled with multiple hieroglyphs. I feel as if I'm seeing a plane of existence sandwiched between realities.

The web grows until it completely surrounds me. I see it as if from the inside of a filmy bubble. I ask if I might get a closer look, and immediately it moves closer, allowing me to get a clearer view of the symbols held within the cells of the web.

Each cell contains multiple linear stick figures that remind me of petroglyphs—simple eye, human, and animal forms. The human figures are all turned right, facing the animals. The eyes number between two and six for each cell. Somehow I know that each cell represents a community of interplanetary species and the notion of universal co-existence.

I hear a very loud and persistent message: "We're here, everywhere, all the time." And the name of the experience comes to me like a passing sigh: "Synchronicity."

The waking experience I describe in my journal was a symbolic visit and a collective message from many benevolent presences in the universe. They didn't tell me where they were from specifically, but I got the feeling they were from disparate locations and dimensions.

Each eye in the painting represents an entity. The human figures are, well, humans, and the animals are representatives of the natural world in which we live. In each cell of the web, the figure faces the animal, symbolizing our relationship to the natural world. The web, meanwhile, represents co-existence, which joins us to all that is. We are not alone. The beings (and I count my guides among them) that exist in other realms are forms of inter-planetary or inter-dimensional life.

We are all part of a larger cosmic community, the web of creation that runs throughout the universe and through all things. Whoever the entities are, they are here right now. "We're here, everywhere, all the time," they said, and I felt their presence as surely as I would feel yours if I were talking to you. I knew that this was a long-time relationship. These were not new arrivals—they were beings that had been with humankind since the beginning of our time on this planet.

Why doesn't everyone see these beings? Are they deliberately hiding? Not at all! A lot of folks see them, children especially, because they've shown themselves and communicated with us down through the ages. Each age interprets their appearance according to the beliefs of the time—as angels, apparitions, the voices of the gods pouring into the willing ear, spirit guides, or ETs. Take your pick.

Sometimes we're taught *not to* look by the powers that be who say that inter-dimensional beings do not exist. When we dismiss from our minds the possibility of other-worldly entities living among us, we are closing ourselves off from direct channels of communication. Our beliefs influence and alter our perceptions, so they can close our psychic eyes and ears as well as open them.

The universe finds many ways to interact with us. Synchronicity is another way for Source to communicate or to send us a message. I think it works somewhat like the inner workings of an infinite cosmic clock. Uncountable gears of action, intent, time, and space work together in a multi-dimensional framework. Every gear is notched into another. The movement of the tiniest gear will eventually affect the largest. Every once in awhile, the cuckoo bird pops out for a brief song and voilá! Synchronistic events occur.

Synchronicity sometimes seems magical. A table you need shows up in the back alley. A friend talks about something you have been thinking about, though you haven't mentioned it to her. A song comes on the radio that answers a question you have been pondering. Events converge with thoughts. Sometimes the most insignificant things gain meaning when synchronicities occur. Their existence seems to support the idea that there are no meaningless coincidences, only meaningful ones.

Synchronicity makes you pay attention.

Synchronicity may seem arranged, as if someone has been watching and waiting for the right moment to bring elements of thought and event together. But it isn't set up. We call events into being, beckoning them in with thought and imagination, and Source responds. When they happen, synchronicities remind us of our magic, our ability to manifest, and our connection with invisible worlds.

I think of synchronicities as breadcrumbs my guides throw in my path. They lead me on from one step to another. I see them best when I'm open and aware—in the moment—and allow myself to be led. When I'm in the flow of life, when I'm not struggling, synchronicity happens more frequently. Or perhaps I allow myself to notice it more.

However it works, synchronicity reassures and delights me. To some degree, it also strikes me with a kind of awe. When synchronicity is a really striking event, something momentous, I think of all the thousands of tiny things that happened to lead to the moment—the seemingly unrelated things that brought those elements or lives together in that place at that time.

Sometimes you meet someone whose personality and interests resonate so closely with your own essence that it seems that all the world conspired to make the meeting happen. Your lives converge like the ripples of two stones thrown into an ocean. This is synchronicity too. I recall being at an experiential workshop in Canada. In one exercise, I was paired with a man who had come all the way from Northern California to attend. He turned out to be an intuitive healer practicing through chiropractic work. In this particular part of the workshop, we were to look into our exercise-partner's eyes. Doug and I looked deeply at each other and I suddenly felt like an alien who, after years of aching loneliness, had met someone from the same home planet. Tears began to stream down his face and I could tell he felt the same. Our companion souls happened to have converged there, at that time, and happened to be paired for this profound exercise. The gears that were set in motion brought us together to give both of us the message that we are not alone in our strange world.

Synchronicity may, at times, feel like a kind of telepathy or clairvoyance—and it is. We think of someone we have not seen for years, the phone rings, and it is that very person. These events make sense if we consider that we are all part of the same vast consciousness.

The idea of telepathy makes some people uncomfortable. They imagine that if a telepath is nearby, their every thought is exposed, or that the telepath is probing their dirty laundry basket without permission. Nope. The thing about telepathy is that it thrives on respect—I don't go rushing pell-mell into your thoughts because it would be an invasion of your privacy.

Unfiltered telepathy may be experienced as a continual whispering sound, a kind of static, that can drive you batty if you don't learn to let your focus move away from it. I can't help but overhear some thoughts, however, because they are broadcast out into the environment. If the thought is passionate, it will increase in pitch, like a voice rising over the ambient background noise of a crowded room. Then it's hard not to hear it.

In some circumstances, people really welcome telepathy. If someone can't speak or find words to express themselves, telepathy can be a tremendous relief. Many people are conscious of a brief telepathy when they look into someone's eyes and know what they are thinking or feeling. It's often important that people feel understood beyond the limitations of what they can say about it.

Telepathy and empathy are closely allied. They both depend on the ability to put oneself aside, and, in a very true sense, to understand—to stand under—and allow another to come through. Both telepathy and empathy have their place in the toolbox of healing, and both can be useful in gaining a deeper understanding of a problem.

I once encountered a woman with Alzheimer's in the dreamtime. Even though it appeared to others that her mind was "gone," I could sense that she was in there somewhere. She was trapped in a body that had disconnected from her mind. She knew perfectly well what she wanted to say or do, but her body seemed to no longer know how to "decode" and act according to her thoughts. Imagine wanting to say potatoes, going to the part of your brain that stored the word for those small brown tubers, and coming across another word instead. You know it's wrong, but your mouth just won't say *potato*. This woman knew that she couldn't remember the names or uses of everyday objects—or how to perform the simplest of tasks. She was totally aware of the misfired signals and could see perfectly well how those around her pitied her.

"How do you remember what to make for dinner?" she asked. "Or remember your kids, who act like dogs that whine and push their empty bowls at you so you remember to feed them?" What a sad question! I could feel her isolated, frustrated, burdened sadness. Through telepathy, I was able to give her a hug and acknowledge the continued presence of her intelligence and perceptions.

We're in constant communication with other forms of consciousness, as they are with us. It is no more strange to sense thought (telepathy) than it is to sense emotion (empathy), and in fact it's an innate ability in humans. A mother senses that her child is in danger. People in love know each other's thoughts. When we focus on someone, especially when that focus is shaped by love, we tune ourselves into them. Imagine then what could happen to the human race if we felt this one-ness, this love and compassion for everybody?

Animals are in communication with us also. I remember as a girl walking with a friend in a grassy field about the size of a football stadium. I was telling her that we could talk to animals with our minds. "Well then," she said, pointing to the other end of the field, where a squirrel was rooting around in the grass. "Can you get that squirrel over *there* to come over *here?*" I hadn't tried anything like that before, but I sent out a request asking the squirrel if he would be willing to come over. He sat up and turned our way. Then he started to leap towards us, never stopping until he had one little paw on my shoe. He stopped then, sat up on his haunches, and looked straight up into my face. I looked back at him, thanked him, and sent him the message that he could go. He scampered off, and my friend's jaw dropped.

As much as we have taken on the hypnosis of separation, we cannot exist except in relationship with both natural and psychic worlds. We are part of something larger. We know this. We know that we are not the whole of things, but we know equally well that we are part of them. We belong to the whole, and it belongs to us.

Synchronicities remind us that our thoughts, the inhabitants of psychic life, are heard and responded to by their neighbors—the thoughts and emotions of other entities that exist in our universe. Starting with our interior world we participate in the creation of the outer world— what it is like, and what comes into being there. Matter depends on thought and emotion to give it form.

Knowing this can bring us to a greater mindfulness of the images and words that we project with our thoughts. They affect others and the environment in which we all live. If we knew each other's thoughts and sensed our communion with everything around us, we would find that synchronicity is not an anomaly, but a constant flowing together of thought and event that is occurring at every moment. We would find that meaningful coincidence is not the exception, but the rule. Most of all, we would truly know the magic of our thoughts and the extent of our mental communion with each other, the physical world, and the spirit and energy realms that are trying to talk to us.

CHAPTER 10

THE GRID

journal entry
Wednesday, June 24, 2004

I'm immersed in darkness. My body is vibrating at a particular frequency—a constant droning hummmmmmmmmmmmm. Shapes and symbols hover before me, grouped in series of threes.

As I study the symbols, I notice that my body is vibrating at one rate and my feet at another. The soles of my feet feel like they are on fire. What begins as a localized intense hurt soon grows into excruciating pain. Unable to bear it any longer, I take a step forward.

With one simple step, I find myself in a wondrous, intricate, grid-like web of interwoven silver light strands. The shimmering Grid extends beyond my view, stretching off into the receding darkness. Close by, I can see that where the strands intersect, lights are glinting and sparkling.

I freeze, not daring to come into contact with this network. I haven't a clue where I am, or what the potential hazards could be. I decide it's best to just hold space, stay in the moment, and take in every detail I can.

I see that each strand is slightly different from its mates, both in thickness and luminosity. The intersecting points vary in degrees of glint and sparkle. Each emits its own sound like a tuning fork—a note so clear and pure you can feel it vibrating through your being.

I am completely surrounded by these strands of silver frequencies when the message comes: "The soul crossover is shifting. It can be disorienting not just for the ghosts, but for the guides, too."

Generally, I don't see The Grid when I help someone cross over. The concept of it is not familiar to me at all.

When I have a dream that reveals different planes of reality or different dimensions, things are represented to me as they are to you in your dreams—in familiar forms of sight and sound and scent. Dreams speak to me in a language of the senses. Other realities are presented in visual terms—like The Grid's beams of light and glittering star-like points—that I can understand and absorb in the waking world. In my dream, The Grid may have been a closer approximation of another plane of existence than I was used to, but it still wasn't the "reality" of that dimension. It was a translation.

My dreams don't come with an explanatory text. When someone asked me what the intersections of the light threads were, I didn't really have an answer. They were themselves. I could have made up something about trajectories of space and time, or imagined that each intersection was a different universe—but I really didn't know. There was no authority telling me what it was I was seeing. I was provided with only the vaguest of clues about my vision, plus a wordless feeling-sense that resonates on an emotional level.

My general understanding of The Grid is this: Permeating all matter is a vibrant, continually changing web of energy. Everything in the material world has life and consciousness—humans, trees, stones, water, buildings, mountains, viruses, each planet and sun, each speck of dust. We are joined to everything around us by the underlying energy of life that we share with all incarnation, all material being.

The intricate web in my dream was a representation of the underlying energy reality of form. Every thread and every point at which they met quivered with vibrancy of being. The Grid was changing ceaselessly, shifting between thought, emotion, action, and reaction. The star-like intersections slipped along the strands of light like dewdrops on a spider's web.

Had I asked why I didn't see other dimensions in their true form, I could not have gotten a better answer than the one at the end of the dream: "The soul crossover is shifting. It can be disorienting not just for the ghosts, but for the guides, too." Perhaps the message was telling me that I would be so disoriented that I would lose my bearings and my job as soul guide would suffer while I stared agog at the powerful, raw magnificence of other realities in their pure form. The Grid in my dream was only a taste, but as much of one as I could take in at the time. Though I kicked myself later for being so untrusting, it was probably a good thing that I didn't dare to touch the strands of light or try to move further into the framework. The potential for wormhole travel, time collapse, and multilayered timelines was potent.

Is this what it looks like to someone as they cross over? My curiosity was piqued. What would have happened if I had walked into the web? Where would I have gone? I wasn't sure I would ever find out. There was nothing to do but wait. Not long after the dream, I did see The Grid again—this time in waking reality. It was an ordinary day of pleasant socializing, and I was with a group of people. I looked across the room to see one of the walls dissolve, revealing the shimmering Grid. I was mesmerized. Who wouldn't be? I was itching to go over and touch it this time, and then I remembered where I was. I figured it would have made for an awkward social moment if I had walked into the wall and disappeared into another dimension, so I stopped myself and tried to act normal. That meant not staring at the wall like a demented cat. It was really hard. Foiled again! This time by etiquette.

I thought I might never get the chance to explore The Grid, and maybe that's so, but recently I had a dream. I was looking at a small portion of The Grid, an orbital bit that had opened on the floor by my feet. One friend stood behind my right shoulder and another by my left. "Touch it!" they both said, nudging me forward. "Go ahead. Touch it!" So I did. It was spongy, and resisted the pressure of my hands with the same electromagnetic energy that I recognized as that which I used in astral flight.

Several months after I saw The Grid, I dreamt of passing through planes of reality. Again, I can't speak to exactly what those realities are; I can only describe their visual representation, the sensations that I felt, and my personal interpretations.

I was surrounded by a black void, suspended in that deep endless black space where there's no evident up or down. A translucent pane of pink appeared before me, thin as glass, and I began to move through it as one would step through the liquid sheet of a waterfall. I felt a hum of vibration that reverberated with the molecules in whichever vertical slice of my body was touching the plane.

I stretched out my hands before me. I hadn't completely stepped through the pink plane when my outstretched fingers encountered a similar dimensional plane of pale green. Again the vibration changed and again the molecules within that vertical slice of my body reverberated with the plane through which it passed. By then, my body was split into several vertical slices of experience, each vibrating at a slightly different frequency. There were vertical bits exposed to the black void, a vertical slice within the pink plane, and another in the green.

It seemed I was not done yet. My furthest outstretched fingers encountered a blue plane. I sensed yet another vibration, a different sort of hum. It was as if three different electrical currents were present and coursing through specific sections of my body. It was a curious sensation.

This was new. I wanted to play. I felt none of the trepidation I had felt when I saw the magnificence of The Grid. Here were smaller slices, the jungle-gyms of consciousness, inviting me to explore. I plunged my hands and body through the panes, feeling the tingling sensations that were part of each color. I jumped back and forth between them, laughing with the childish joy of adventure. The sensations played themselves out in happy little currents throughout my body.

Two nights later, I dreamt again of moving through other dimensions. I was in a room, looking at a translucent mirror. I knew that this was a dimensional plane dividing waking reality and the dreaming reality. I went to the mirror, and carefully extended my fingers towards it. Again, it was a pliable, liquid, vertical plane, no thicker than a sheet of glass. I stepped through, and felt again the differing frequencies and played with the sensations of the dimensions.

A little over a month later, I had entered the borderland of consciousness. My awareness expanded upwards, and I saw three horizontal planes of reality extending beyond my vision in all directions. One layer hovered one or two feet above me. Further up still, another one or two feet higher than the last, a second layer hovered. These three realities—the two above me and the one I was occupying—were sandwiched together, yet they were vibrating slightly out of sync with one another. Each layer oscillated left and right, trying to fit with the others, flowing downward in an attempt to come together by finding the right niche or groove so it could lock into place. I wonder if this might be a clue as to why spirits and energy beings do not appear clearly to everyone. Perhaps being psychic is like having a kind of double vision—one set of eyes seeing the material world and one set having peripheral vision that perceives an alternate reality that is slightly "to the side" of the physical.

I usually see ghosts hovering one or two feet above the ground, so it is interesting that the heights in my lucid dream were the same. Perhaps the two planes above me were the realities that are accessible to all human beings. The first, closest to the reality of the five senses, would be the ethereal, where ghosts dwell and guides speak, where physical healing takes place on an energetic level, and where dreams interact with daily life. The second plane could well be the astral, where the restraints of time and space are completely released, where spirits are escorted to Love's Light. These are purely speculations on my part. They are the interpretations I give to experiences that are in many ways beyond words. Something is always lost in translation when you put names to visions, but it's still human to try.

Those dreams were an introduction of sorts. "Here is what the planes look like," the dreams said. "Now we'll show you how you move between them." In the next week, I learned exactly how I travel through the planes and appear at a destination in another dimension. A twinkle of dust coalesced in the darkness as a seam in reality appeared before me. I pulled the sides apart to pass through, and as I did so a protective, translucent, glowing orb enclosed me. I squeezed through the seam and emerged on the other side, where the glass-like orb dissolved. Here I was in some other place or some other time.

In my travels, I took great caution not to disturb anything too drastically. True non-interference is not possible, because every movement through space and time alters something.

Just how this works was demonstrated to me in a dream I had in 2003. I saw the energy structure that underlies form as an elastic sheet, and sensed the stress that occurs in objects when structure is manipulated on an energy level. Travel through dimensions creates a molecular imprint, like the impression left on the surface of taffy when you poke it. The molecules stretch in the area where the seam has been passed through, and the stretching increases with every visit. That's important to know. Astral travel has an effect and can't be taken lightly. Moreover, when you travel through space and time, it's possible to visit cultures that are working on their own evolution. The general directive on the Night Shift is non-interference at that level. In general, it's better to not allow yourself to be seen. Your visible presence in their world may alter the course of events radically, so you must take caution wherever you go. Movement into early earthly life, for instance, may affect our world today. As we have learned, time is simultaneous. Past and future exist in the now and the now exists in them. Your own past and future lives are accessible. Your experiences in another life affect this one, because they are both you. All the lives that you create are being lived now because linear time is an illusion. All time is now.

An illness or trauma in another life can be held in the body in this life as a symptom. As strange as it sounds, you can visit yourself in another life, heal something there, and come back to this physical reality to find that the symptom has disappeared. It will have disappeared in *all* of your simultaneous lives.

I was able to experience such a healing during a past life regression—or should I say "alternate life exploration"—with Carolyn. During this particular session, I was dealing with issues around my neck. Since I could remember, I'd hated anything around my neck—scarves especially. I could tolerate loose turtlenecks, but I detested anything that could be tied like a scarf or a cravat.

As I relaxed and entered a meditative state, Carolyn guided me deeper and deeper into the layers of my body. "Where do you feel discomfort in your body now?" she asked. "What feelings come to the surface when you go there? Do you see colors? Describe them. What feelings are associated with them? Do images come up? Sounds? Smells?"

Slowly, I became aware that I was in a different timeframe. I experienced myself as a light-skinned but very tanned male in my late 20s, taller than I am now, and physically strong. I was no longer in the western hemisphere; the sun was beating down with fierce intensity and the parched air was clogged with heat and dust. I was trapped in a stockade with a number of other people, all of us held captive there. Heavy iron collars were fastened around our necks and the long chains attached to them tethered us to thick walls. I could feel the deep bonds of family and culture—blood and history—that I had with my fellow prisoners.

Then I found myself outside the pen, free to go, even though I still had the collar and chain around my neck. Unwilling to abandon the others, I walked back towards the stockade, but they waved me back and pointed into the distance, making it clear that I *must* leave them, even though our hearts were tied together. I felt overwhelmingly guilty that I was the only person set free. My heart and throat constricted with sorrow and shame. "I should be in there with them," I thought.

Suddenly, from my present life, I understood. Survivor's guilt from that lifetime had kept me "collared" through other lives. I realized that I could change my perceptions and feelings in *that* incarnation from the viewpoint of *this* one. I could let go of the self-blame I had constructed as I stood looking back at my loved ones.

The young man that I was then truly accepted that it was part of his destiny to walk away from the prison, that this was his path. He—I—embraced my journey and the emotional burden I had carried with me through lifetimes was lifted. The strangling iron collar of guilt loosened and fell to the ground as I turned to walk away. The heavy chain of negative self-judgment crumpled in a heap beside it. As I lay on Carolyn's table, I felt the shifts of this new perception through my body in a buoyant release. It seemed as if my heart was physically lighter, and I understood that there was no judgment save the one I had put on myself.

Some problems seem to recur through several lifetimes. In the one I live here and now, I have had to deal with issues around accepting my path. So this lifetime is perhaps not so different from the one I lived (or *still* live, apparently) as that young man who walked away from the prison.

It's been difficult because I have for much of my life felt so different. I'm not standing outside a stockade this time around, but I feel at times as if I'm apart from mainstream society. A large part of it came from having grown up in a place where there was so little information about psychic phenomena, and certainly no earthly teachers to be found.

I'm glad, in retrospect, that I didn't have access to the written wisdom of the past, to a cultural or spiritual tradition that encouraged direct contact with the divine. It was hard to feel so alone, but still I'm glad because I had to look inside myself for all the answers that I couldn't find in the tiny, conservative library of my home town, or the straightforward and down-to-earth values of the human family and community into which I was born. The isolation helped me, when I finally came to accept and embrace my path, to claim my experience more fully as my own.

That isolation is diminishing over time. Things are changing. There is so much more information available now that it's easy to consult literally hundreds of spiritual teachings and traditions through books, film, TV, and the Internet. There are many thousands, if not millions, of people in the world who have shared the direct experience of alternate realities, and who today live with that strange intermingling of psychic and material life. People are talking, even in conservative industrial towns, about the possibilities of human consciousness, yet the message is always the same: Look within. Trust yourself. Love. What you believe you will get is what you will get. Pay attention to your thoughts. Incarnation is an art.

We are living in a very special time in history. We are free to speak of our direct contact with universal powers and our own divinity in a new way. We are beginning to understand our free will, and the agonizing and beautiful responsibility that it brings.

In other lives, I've died protecting the validity of human beings' personal, intimate, real relationship with their own divinity. Earth is telling us, our bodies are telling us, and our hearts are telling us that there is a healing that has to take place. We all know it. We must fix the misalignment in our relationships to Earth, to each other, and within ourselves.

Maybe if we all just admitted our experiences to each other, we'd find that extrasensory perceptions, communications with spirits and animals, energy healing, and astral travel are not so far out after all. Maybe paranormal *is* normal.

That's why I'm here—to lend my voice to the chorus of voices speaking up to share what we know first-hand and to offer a forum for others to come forward and speak their truth. I'm not alone in this endeavor. There are many like me who work in invisible dimensions to help other souls. I don't know them all, of course. We tend to stick to ourselves, and come out of the proverbial closet only when we can no longer endure hiding. But we know we must speak up for what we think is right—love and light.

Love is the key. There are so many things that we can find that separate us—oceans and cultures, opinions, all the flaws and foibles of being human. We are at a point when we need to find what joins us as individuals to the human community. There is only one thing that binds us together in our journey through incarnation and it is love. Let us meet in the dreamtime not as separate individuals, but as spirits embraced by our mutual love. Let go of fear, of personal glory, of the false honor of revenge. Be humbled in the love that holds the universe together. We are part of it. We are it.

In this life, one of my greatest joys has been the experience of motherhood. I think about not only my own children, but also the children all over the Earth who look to us, the parents and adults in their lives, for guidance—and they're like little sponges. They come here into their own incarnation with full spirits, eager to learn what they are in themselves, and to learn how they fit into the human community. It is a sacred honor, I think, to help them, to listen to them, and to guide them with gentle openness. It is important for us to accept the amazing brilliance of our children and to help them feel comfortable and unafraid in their own skins.

Each of us has our personal experience. I've struggled during the writing of this book with finding the right word to define myself. Am I shaman, psychic, medium, mystic? How do I find just the right term to encompass my experience and my consciousness? In the end, I come again and again to the pronouncement of my guides: I'm a fringe dweller. I live in both the material and the spirit worlds, and I dwell in the places where they meet and overlap. Aside from names or definitions, it is what it is.

A large part of my motivation in writing this book, and in coming out of the psychic closet, is to encourage others, children and adults, to trust their inner knowing and embrace their unique way. Human consciousness is evolving so fast that it is important now for us to be open and honest about our personal contact and experience with Source.

Before I go, I share with you the advice my guides gave to me:

Put your gifts out there. Each of you has one gift, or more likely several, and the world needs them. Acknowledge and embrace the creativity of your being. Practice your art, whatever form it may take.

Share. Sharing is not only giving, it is also learning how to receive. It is an intention and action of graceful exchange. Let us share our spirits, our creation, and our abundant compassion. Sharing is embodied in the concept of Namaste, an ancient greeting performed with palms held together and a slight bow. When you acknowledge someone with a Namaste, you are saying, "The divine in me greets the divine in you."

Do not be attached to the outcome. Spirit may lead you in surprising directions. Go with it. Allow. Trust. Loosen the reins of control enough to allow the path to open up before you. You are an explorer, and sometimes you won't know what is around the next corner or bend in the river. Let the curious, joyful child in you free. Life is a delicious mystery, an unfolding discovery, a quest.

I imagine a world in which we allow for each of us to freely be a member of the divinely conceived human family living in intimate relationship with inter-dimensional beings, animals, plants, minerals, and the soil that feeds us. In that world, we will have come back from our adventures and our wanderings and our separation to the light and to each other. At long last, we will be home, embraced by the union that is our destiny.

ABOUT THE AUTHOR

Photograph © Karen Learmonth

Monica Holy is an artist, psychic, medium, spirit guide, and mother of two. She has worked in animation, photography, and typography for film and television. For most of her life she kept her psychic and spiritual life a secret. She now feels the time is right to share her story, and hopes it will help others understand their own journey through life. This is her first book. She lives in Vancouver, BC. For more information, visit the Web site *www.thefringedweller.com*.